Dear Father, open the eyes of their understanding that they may know Your great love and the exceeding greatness of Your power that is within them. Show them Your heart, Lord. Make them see the life You want them to live.

—James R. Riddle

THE COMPLETE PERSONALIZED PROMISE BIBLE ON

HEALTH AND HEALING

EVERY HEALING SCRIPTURE PROMISE,

PERSONALIZED AND WRITTEN

AS A PRAYER JUST FOR YOU

by

James R. Riddle

Harrison House
Tulsa, OK

Unless otherwise indicated all verses are taken from the *New King James Version* of the Bible. Used by permission.

10 09 08 07   10 9 8 7 6 5 4 3

The Complete Personalized Promise Bible on Health and Healing:
Every Healing Scripture Promise,
Personalized and Written as a Prayer Just for You
ISBN 13: 978-1-57794-840-7
ISBN 10: 1-57794-840-8
Copyright © 2007 by James R. Riddle
6930 Gateway East
El Paso, Texas 79915

Published by Harrison House, Inc.
P.O. Box 35035
Tulsa, Oklahoma 74153

CONTENTS

DEDICATION

I dedicate this book to all of you who are facing incurable diseases. Don't give up hope. God can heal what the doctors cannot. It's time to dig your heels in and be a scrapper for the Word. Make the quality choice to purge the poison of negative emotions, doubt-filled words, and unhealthy foods from your life. This may be the most difficult time you have ever faced, but you can win this fight. Engraft the words of this book into your spirit and place your heel on the devil's neck! Remember: "All things are possible to him who believes" (Mark 9:23).

Know that my prayers are with you, and I'm looking forward to hearing the testimony of your healing.

INTRODUCTION

Shalom.

Shalom is one of the most beautiful words in existence. It literally means "nothing missing, nothing broken."[1] It also means to be completely whole in every way. *Shalom* is perfect peace.[2]

Our Lord Jesus is the Prince of Shalom. (Isa. 9:6.) His greatest desire for you is that you live in health, prosperity, joy, and absolute fulfillment in every area of your life. If even a small part of your life is lacking any part of these, He feels it. You must realize that your Lord loves you with a perfect love. He cherishes every breath you take. He counts the very hairs on your head and holds as precious every one.

Examine this thought for a moment. The Word says that our "hope does not disappoint, because the love of God has been poured out in our hearts by the Holy Spirit who [has been] given to us" (Rom. 5:5). Now add to your meditation of this thought that faith is the substance of things hoped for and that faith must work by love. (Heb. 11:1; Gal. 5:6.) How does faith come? By hearing the Word continually until we realize that the promise is for us. (Rom. 10:17.) How can we be disappointed? When we don't know the love that God has for us and how willing He is to fulfill His Word in our lives.

You see, no matter how much I tell you that God loves you and wants you well, it does you no good if you don't believe it and act upon it by using your faith.

The Word implicitly says that the Holy Spirit who is within you reveals to you just how much the Father loves you. (1 Cor. 2:10-12; Rom. 5:5; Gal. 4:6.) This is a promise from God. Therefore, I am sure beyond any shadow of doubt that as you read these pages the light of His love will dawn on you, the Holy Spirit will open the eyes of your understanding, and you will know what Jesus did for you.

I personally believe that if you recognize love in its fullest measure, no sin, sickness, disease, or malady will ever hold you in bondage again. You will stand up and joyfully proclaim, "My Father loves me! I am His precious child and He holds me close to His heart. I do not belong to Satan. I am not a child of bondage. I am a child of God and He has set me free!"

Ask yourself this question and give it an honest answer: *What was it that moved Jesus with compassion when He walked this earth?*

You don't have to know a whole lot about the Bible to know that Jesus healed hurting people wherever He went. Matthew 14:14 says, "When Jesus went out He saw [the] great multitude; and He was moved with compassion for them, and healed their sick." He lived to see the joy in people's eyes when their leprosy was healed, when their blind eyes were opened, when fever left them, and when cripples walked. He brought hope to those who had no hope left. When doctors could do no more for the sick, Jesus would come, lay His hands on them, and set them free.

Did you know that Jesus is the same yesterday, today, and forever? (Heb. 13:8.) That same love that reached out to those people is now reaching out to you. He rejoices when you take Him at His Word and receive your healing by faith.

~ NO GREATER LOVE ~

According to the Word, God is all three persons of the Trinity—God the Father, God the Son, and God the Holy Spirit (1 John 5:7;

John 10:30), and His love for us is so great that it is beyond our ability to understand or experience its fullness. That makes me think of the words of Jesus (God the Son) when He said that there is no greater love than when a man will lay down his life for a friend. (John 15:13.) Do you want to know how much He loves you? Read these verses:

> "I am the good shepherd. The good shepherd gives His life for the sheep. But a hireling, he who is not the shepherd, one who does not own the sheep, sees the wolf coming and leaves the sheep and flees; and the wolf catches the sheep and scatters them. The hireling flees because he is a hireling and does not care about the sheep. I am the good shepherd; and I know My sheep, and am known by My own. As the Father knows Me, even so I know the Father; and I lay down My life for the sheep. And other sheep I have which are not of this fold; them also I must bring, and they will hear My voice; and there will be one flock and one shepherd. Therefore My Father loves Me, because I lay down My life that I may take it again. No one takes it from Me, but I lay it down of Myself. I have power to lay it down, and I have power to take it again. This command I have received from My Father."
>
> John 10:11–18

Do you see the love in these remarkable words of Jesus? God so loved us that He sent His Son Jesus to die for us. (John 3:16.) But what stands out to me in this passage is the statement "No one takes it from me, but I lay it down of Myself." Jesus was not a martyr; He was a willing sacrifice. He was never helpless. What He did for us, He did willingly, as an act of pure love.

There is no greater love in existence than the love that Jesus has for you. The writer of Hebrews tells us that for the joy that was set before Jesus, He "endured the cross, despising the shame" (Heb. 12:2). He suffered willingly because He always saw something before Him that filled Him full of joy. He chose to allow all of that torment and misery because of something wonderful that He saw was going to come from it. Let's examine, on a scriptural basis, exactly what it was that was set before Him.

First of all, it is utterly essential that we realize that Jesus always had a choice. His life was His to pick up and lay down as He chose. That means at any moment He could have stopped the pain. But He never gave in. He stood there for you and for me—for the whole world (John 3:16)—but let's take it one step further, to a more personal level.

When they punched your Lord's face, it was your blows He was taking. When they spat on Him and mocked Him, He was enduring your shame. When they beat His precious body with that whip, it was your body that should have been there. But He withstood it all. He didn't complain. He didn't plead for mercy. He just took every blow for you.

At any moment He could have stopped it. He could have said that the price was too high to endure such suffering. His life was His to pick up and lay down as He chose. But for the joy set before Him, He let the abuse and the torture go on. He chose not to stop it.

Not even the anguish of the cross or hell's deepest pit could make Him give in. He willingly endured it all because of the joy He saw before Him. What was the joy? What was it that elated Jesus so much in the midst of suffering?

~ RECEIVE IT BY FAITH ~

Did you know that you were chosen before the beginning of time? (2 Thess. 2:13.) That means that Jesus knew you before time began. He knew you as He walked this earth. And He knew you as He endured your pain. The Word says that when His soul was made an offering for sin, He saw His seed. (Isa. 53:10.) Who is Jesus' seed? You are. The joy that was set before Him was *you*.

With every step He took, He saw you. When they beat Him with that whip, He saw you. When they drove those nails into His precious hands, He saw you. It was love for you that held Him to that cross— and that same love is reaching out to you every day of your life.

So what did all that suffering accomplish? I cannot say it better than what the Holy Spirit said through the prophet Isaiah.

Who has believed our report? And to whom has the arm of the LORD been revealed? For He shall grow up before Him as a tender plant, and as a root out of dry ground. He has no form or comeliness; and when we see Him, there is no beauty that we should desire Him. He is despised and rejected by men, a Man of sorrows and acquainted with grief. And we hid, as it were, our faces from Him; He was despised, and we did not esteem Him. Surely He has borne our griefs and carried our sorrows; yet we esteemed Him stricken, smitten by God, and afflicted. But He was wounded for our trans-gressions, He was bruised for our iniquities; the chastisement for our peace was upon Him, and by His stripes we are healed. All we like sheep have gone astray; we have turned, every one, to his own way; and the LORD has laid on Him the iniquity of us all. He was oppressed and He was afflicted, yet He opened not His mouth; He was led as a lamb to the slaughter, and as a sheep before its shearers is silent, so He opened not His mouth. He was taken from prison and from judgment, and who will declare His generation? For He was cut off from the land of the living; for the transgressions of My people He was stricken. And they made His grave with the wicked—but with the rich at His death, because He had done no violence, nor was any deceit in His mouth. Yet it pleased the LORD to bruise Him; He has put Him to grief. When You make His soul an offering for sin, He shall see His seed, He shall prolong His days, and the pleasure of the LORD shall prosper in His hand. He shall see the labor of His soul, and be satisfied. By His knowledge My righteous Servant shall justify many, for He shall bear their iniquities. Therefore I will divide Him a portion with the great, and He shall divide the spoil with the strong, because He poured out His soul unto death, and He was numbered with the transgressors, and He bore the sin of many, and made intercession for the transgressors.

Isaiah 53:1–12

Jesus died for you to bring you *shalom*. Broken relationship and fellowship with God has now been restored. Sickness is now healed. In place of poverty, there is abundant provision. Everything that you need to live in health, prosperity, joy, and absolute fulfillment is now yours in Christ Jesus. He paid an awesome price so you could have every good promise of His Word. (2 Cor. 1:20.) All that He asks is that you receive it by faith.

~ *ARE YOU WILLING?* ~

As I read and reread the promises of healing contained in the pages of this book, I was ever-increasingly amazed at how much the love of God was expressed, but a sobering fact emerged over and over again. That fact is that no matter how much God loves us, He will not heal us just because we want to be healed. He expects us to receive our healing according to the pattern and guidelines He has placed in His Word.

Our words, attitudes, emotions, and overall lifestyles play a major role in the receiving of what God has for us. We cannot reason against the Word because of our circumstances. Our circumstances are not the final authority. If we still feel sick after we've prayed in faith, it does not mean that it is not God's will for us to be well. We must continue in faith, knowing that by faith and patience we will receive the promise. (Heb. 6:12.)

Just imagine what it was like to be there with Jesus and watch as the leprous man came up to Him and said, "Lord, if You are willing, You can make me [well]," then seeing Jesus, with compassion in His eyes, reach out and hold him, saying, "I am willing; be cleansed" (Matt. 8:2,3). The man knew that Jesus *could,* he just didn't know if He *would.* All it took for the leprous man to receive was that word, "I am willing." That same word is for you.

Remember, all of God's promises in Him, are yes and amen. (2 Cor. 1:20.) God is more than willing to pour His healing power through your body and make every cell work as it should. But the ball is in your court. It is up to you to work the Word in faith.

Several times in the Bible Jesus tells those who are healed, "Be of good cheer; your faith has made you well. Go in *shalom.*" We have seen that faith comes by continually hearing the Word until you recognize that it is for you. Once you have that faith, couple it with patience. If you do that, you can receive your healing every time!

HOW TO USE THIS BOOK

In this book there are hundreds of Scripture verses that contain God's promises for your healing. Meditate on them. Speak them to yourself. Ask your heavenly Father to enlighten the eyes of your understanding. Know what belongs to you as a child of the living God and commit yourself to walk in the light of what you know.

Each Scripture is followed by a prayer and a "Declaration of Faith" based upon the given verse. Read the Scripture verse to build your faith, pray the prayer from your heart, and speak the "Declaration of Faith" aloud as a positive affirmation of that promise for your life.

Each prayer is a relationship prayer. They speak to God on a very personal level. They will bring you into closeness with your Father God. You will be at His very throne pouring your heart out to Him. Elaborate all you want. Tell Him how you feel, how much you love Him and appreciate all that He has done. Stay in faith and know that He is with you at all times.

You will notice that each "Declaration of Faith" is fully cross-referenced. Each of these references are added so you can understand how the verse harmonizes with the overall message of the Bible. For instance, we may read Deuteronomoy 28:15-68 and summize that God is going to curse us with all kinds of problems if we don't always do the right things. Therefore, the cross-references of Galatians 3:13-16, and the other verses listed, are added to procure understanding that through Jesus we are redeemed from the curse of the law and now have the freedom to enjoy the very opposite of every one of those curses.

Cross-referencing is extremely powerful in establishing key concepts of the Word into our lives. The Bible says, "In the mouth of two or three credible witnesses let every word be established" (Deut. 19:15, author paraphrase). Therefore, each personalized text is complete with at least two establishing cross-references.

It is important that you do not skip over the Word and go straight to the prayers and declarations—they are not what will generate faith. Faith comes by hearing and meditating on the Word. It is only the Word that makes the prayers powerful. When you know the promise and understand it is for you, you can pray with confidence that it will be manifested in your life.

God has given you every promise in this book. They are yours to receive by faith. Read them, pray them, and declare them as your own. Before you do, let's begin with an opening prayer and believe together for your healing.

Father God, I come before You with thanksgiving and praise. You are holy and just, and Your incredible mercy endures forever. I am awed by Your great love for me. I recognize it in all that Jesus did. He lived to do Your will. Therefore, I know that it is Your will to do good and heal all who are oppressed of the devil. I have no doubt, Father, that healing is mine, in Jesus' name.

Father, Your Word says that in Jesus all of Your great and precious promises are for me. By Your Word, I can confidently declare every one of them to be accomplished in my life. I choose to believe, Father. I stand in the face of my circumstances and declare Your Word as the final author-

ity. Jesus bore my sicknesses and carried my pains; the chastisement for my shalom was upon Him, and with the stripes that wounded Him, I am healed. I receive Your healing in my mind and body, in Jesus' name.

Satan, I command you and every devil to take your filthy hands off of me. Your sicknesses, diseases, and maladies shall not reign in me. I am in Christ Jesus and He has set me free!

Body, I command you now, by the authority of God's Word: be healed! I command every cell to work properly. Unhealthy cells, I tell you now that you are flooded with God's healing power. Healing, pour through my body until it is in perfect working order.

Father, I know that Your Word is alive, and powerful, and sharper than any two-edged sword. It has within it the very power of fulfillment. Therefore, I seal the fate of all ailments by declaring it to You now, in Jesus' name!

CHAPTER ONE

GENESIS

GENESIS 20:17

So Abraham prayed to God; and God healed Abimelech, his wife, and his female servants. Then they bore children.

~ PRAYER ~

Father, I thank You for the privilege of having You as my partner in this life. I know that You hear me when I pray and You faithfully answer. Therefore, I stand in the gap for the one in need of healing. (Name them.) Heal them, Father, from the top of their head to the bottom of their feet. May they know that there is a God in heaven who is concerned for their health.

——— *DECLARATION OF FAITH* ———

I am an intercessor for the Lord. I stand in the gap for those troubled by sickness and bring the Word of healing to make them whole. If they are barren, by this verse I have the authority to loose them from bondage that they may bear the children they so desire to have.

(John 14:12; Ezekiel 22:30; Exodus 8:9; Ephesians 6:17,18; Psalm 107:20)

GENESIS 24:1

Now Abraham was old, well advanced in age; and the LORD had blessed Abraham in all things.

~ *PRAYER* ~

Father, I know that the blessing of Abraham is upon me. I am a blessed man/woman made to be a blessing to the world. Sickness and disease have no part in Your blessing. I am blessed in all things, which includes my health. Therefore, I shall live to a ripe old age, praising You for Your goodness every day of my long and abundant life!

—— *DECLARATION OF FAITH* ——

I am blessed in all things and in every way. I do not tolerate sickness in my body, for it is contrary to the blessing of the Lord. Jesus bought me the right to this blessing and I intend to walk in it!

(Galatians 3:13-16; Ephesians 1:3; Isaiah 53:3-5; 2 Peter 1:3)

CHAPTER TWO

EXODUS

Exodus 4:11

So the LORD said to him, "Who has made man's mouth? Or who makes the mute, the deaf, the seeing, or the blind? Have not I, the LORD?"

~ *PRAYER* ~

Father, You know me thoroughly. You know every cell in my body and how it works. You know the origin of anything that would come against me to steal the life that You have called me to live. Therefore, I am fully confident that You will heal me with a perfect healing.

——— *DECLARATION OF FAITH* ———

I serve an omniscient God. He loves me dearly and responds with compassion to my prayers. He sees the sickness that tries to deny me of the life that I have been given. He attacks it with a vengeance and sets me back on the path of victory.

(Psalm 139; John 10:10; Romans 8:31-39)

Exodus 15:26

"If you diligently heed the voice of the LORD your God and do what is right in His sight, give ear to His commandments and keep all His statutes, I will put none of the diseases on you which I have brought on the Egyptians. For I am the LORD who heals you."

~ PRAYER ~

Father, You are my life. There is nothing that I desire more than to have Your companionship. When I hear Your Word, I hear Your voice. It is precious treasure to me and I cling to it with all that is within me. Your statutes and commandments are life to me in abundance. Through them I have knowledge of Your unfailing mercy and grace. I sense Your love, Father. You are my Jehovah Rapha—my healer.[1] Praise be to Your holy name!

——— DECLARATION OF FAITH ———

I have a covenant with God. I diligently listen, giving my complete attention to His Word, and I do what is right in His sight. My ear is open to His voice and I am prepared to follow His commands.

I have His Word that no disease can come upon me which is brought upon the world; for my God is Jehovah Rapha, the God who heals me. He is the Lord of my health.

(Hebrews 8:6; 10:16,17; Deuteronomy 28:1; Isaiah 30:21; 53:5; Psalm 103:1-5)

Exodus 23:25,26

"So you shall serve the LORD your God, and He will bless your bread and your water. And I will take sickness away from the midst of you. No one shall suffer miscarriage or be barren in your land; I will fulfill the number of your days."

~ *PRAYER* ~

Father, thank You for Your Word with its precious promises. In You I am blessed beyond measure. You bless my bread and water and take all sickness away from me. You preserve my offspring and fulfill my number of days in a long and abundant life. You are so awesome, Lord, and You are a pleasure to serve.

——— *DECLARATION OF FAITH* ———

I serve the Lord my God and He blesses my bread and water.

He has taken sickness from my spirit and I am healed in my body.

My children shall live a long, full, and abundant life.

(Young women declare: "I am not barren, nor do I miscarry my babies.")

The Lord fulfills the number of my days on the earth.

(1 Timothy 4:4,5; Ephesians 6:1-3; Psalms 91:16; 103:1-5; Isaiah 46:4; Luke 9:42)

CHAPTER THREE

NUMBERS

NUMBERS 12:10-15

And when the cloud departed from above the tabernacle, suddenly Miriam became leprous, as white as snow. Then Aaron turned toward Miriam, and there she was, a leper. So Aaron said to Moses, "Oh, my lord! Please do not lay this sin on us, in which we have done foolishly and in which we have sinned. Please do not let her be as one dead, whose flesh is half consumed when he comes out of his mother's womb!" So Moses cried out to the LORD, saying, "Please heal her, O God, I pray!" Then the LORD said to Moses, "If her father had but spit in her face, would she not be shamed seven days? Let her be shut out of the camp seven days, and afterward she may be received again." So Miriam was shut out of the camp seven days, and the people did not journey till Miriam was brought in again.

~ *PRAYER* ~

Father, I hold fast to Your mercy. You do not look upon my sin, but You see me through the eyes of grace. Your love for me is stronger than death and as unyielding as the grave. Your forgiveness is everlasting. By Your grace I stand, and by Your grace I am healed. Jesus bore my shame on the cross and by His wounds I am made well.

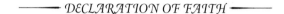

DECLARATION OF FAITH

I am an intercessor in the family of God. When Satan's sickness takes hold of another, I stand in the gap for them and declare their healing. The Lord hears my prayers and responds with tender compassion. I respond to His compassion with obedience as a good son/daughter should. I am quick to obey His requirements and will follow His instructions without fail.

(Romans 5:1,2; Galatians 3:1-5; Hebrews 12:2; Ezekiel 22:30)

CHAPTER FOUR

DEUTERONOMY

DEUTERONOMY 4:40

"You shall therefore keep His statutes and His commandments which I command you today, that it may go well with you and with your children after you, and that you may prolong your days in the land which the LORD your God is giving you for all time."

~ *PRAYER* ~

Father, I choose to be a doer of Your Word. I know the importance of doing what You tell me to do. Your Word is life to me and health to all of my flesh. By following Your precepts, it goes well with me and my children after me, and we live long on this earth which You have given us forever.

—— *DECLARATION OF FAITH* ——

I know, understand, and give my complete attention to the fact that my heavenly Father is the One true God in heaven above and on earth beneath. There is no other.

He is my Father, my Lord, my Master, my Teacher, and my Example.

I obey all of His commands, for by them it goes well with me and with my children after me.

He has engrafted His Word into my heart so that I may prolong my days in a full and abundant life in the land that He has given me as an inheritance for all of eternity.

(Isaiah 43:10,11; 44:6; 45:5,6; 46:4,9; Psalms 91:16; 103:17; Ephesians 5:1,2)

DEUTERONOMY 5:16

"Honor your father and your mother, as the LORD your God has commanded you, that your days may be long, and that it may be well with you in the land which the LORD your God is giving you."

~ PRAYER ~

Father, I thank You for my parents. They birthed me into this world and are worthy to be honored. More importantly, You, Father, have commanded that I honor them. Therefore, I do not look to their imperfections, but I focus on that which is good. I will give honor where honor is due and trust Your Word that it will go well with me and that I will live long in the land.

DECLARATION OF FAITH

I honor my father and mother, as the Lord has commanded me. My days shall be long and it shall go well with me in the land which the Lord my God is giving me.

(Ephesians 6:1-3; Psalm 91:16; Deuteronomy 4:40)

DEUTERONOMY 5:29

Oh, that they had such a heart in them that they would fear Me and always keep all My commandments, that it might be well with them and with their children forever!

~ PRAYER ~

Father, I sense Your heart in Your Word. Like a good Father, You just want Your kids to listen and obey. You don't give commands for the command's sake, but so we can live the abundant life You have called us to. Father, I know that You are tending to my best interests. Your compassion for me is endless and Your heart's desire is to bless me in every way. Therefore, You have my heart completely. I will do what you tell me to do so that it will go well with me and my children after me forever!

—— DECLARATION OF FAITH ——

I have a heart for my Father. I keep His Word and follow His ways. By His precepts, it goes well with me and my children after me.

(Deuteronomy 4:40; Isaiah 46:4; Psalm 103:17)

DEUTERONOMY 5:32,33

"Therefore you shall be careful to do as the LORD your God has commanded you; you shall not turn aside to the right hand or to the left. You shall walk in all the ways which the LORD your God has commanded you, that you may live and that it may be well with you, and that you may prolong your days in the land which you shall possess."

~ *PRAYER* ~

Father, I make my unwavering choice to walk in Your ways. Open the eyes of my understanding that I may know Your Word thoroughly. Engraft Your precepts in the tablet of my heart so that I may live my life the way You have called me to live it. With You as my guide, it shall go well with me and I will live a long, prosperous, and healthy life.

——— *DECLARATION OF FAITH* ———

I walk in all of the ways of God. He is my mentor and the example by which I live.

I obey His every command.

His Word is life to me, and I will obey it so that it may go well with me and that I may live long in the land that He has given me.

(Ephesians 5:1,2; Deuteronomy 28:1; John 15:10-17; Psalm 119:66,68; Isaiah 46:4)

DEUTERONOMY 7:12-16

"Then it shall come to pass, because you listen to these judgments, and keep and do them, that the LORD your God will keep with you the covenant and the mercy which He swore to your fathers. And He will love you and bless you and multiply you; He will also bless the fruit of your womb and the fruit of your land, your grain and your new wine and your oil, the increase of your cattle and the offspring of your flock, in the land of which He swore to your fathers to give you. You shall be blessed above all peoples; there shall not be a male or female barren among you or among your livestock. And the LORD will take away from you all sickness, and will afflict you with none of the terrible diseases of Egypt which you have known, but will lay them on all those who hate you. Also you shall destroy all the peoples whom the LORD your God delivers over to you; your eye shall have no pity on them; nor shall you serve their gods, for that will be a snare to you."

~ *PRAYER* ~

Father, I thank You for our covenant. Thank You for loving me, and blessing me, and multiplying me. Thank You for causing Your anointing to flow through my life so that I have all that I need and more. Thank You for taking all sickness and disease away from me so that I can live my life in health and vitality. You are good to me, Father. I have not earned, nor do I deserve, any of these great blessings based on my own merits, but You give them to me freely. Through Jesus, I am now under Your covenant protection. None of the terrible diseases of the world may cling to me. In Jesus' name, I am made whole in every way!

—— DECLARATION OF FAITH ——

I am blessed above all worldly people.

There is no one, nor is there anything, who is barren in my house.

Everyone in my house is blessed. We live in God's favor and abound in His prosperity.

There is no sickness allowed near my dwelling. The Lord has taken all sickness from me. He does not permit any of the diseases of the world to come upon my household. Instead, they are laid upon my enemies.

(Deuteronomy 28:1-14; Psalm 103:1-5,17; Proverbs 13:22; Exodus 15:26; 23:22)

DEUTERONOMY 12:28

Observe and obey all these words which I command you, that it may go well with you and your children after you forever, when you do what is good and right in the sight of the LORD your God.

~ PRAYER ~

Father, I know that I have a responsibility to live right in this earth. I understand the laws of seedtime and harvest, and that if I sow to my flesh, of the flesh I will reap corruption. Therefore, I will do what is good and right in Your sight. I will not fill my body full of sugar and fat and then expect to live healthy. To the contrary, I will feed it what it needs and care for it as the holy temple in which You dwell. Guide me in my efforts, Father. Give me revelation of Your Word that it may go well with me and with my children after me.

──── DECLARATION OF FAITH ────

I observe and obey the Word of the Lord, and it goes well with me and my children after me forever. I do what is good and right in the sight of God.

(Galatians 6:7-9; Deuteronomy 28:1; 1 Corinthians 3:16,17)

Deuteronomy 28:15-68

[Note: This is the curse that Jesus redeemed you from. Because of what Jesus did for you, you can expect the exact opposite of all that this curse says.]

"But it shall come to pass, if you do not obey the voice of the Lord your God, to observe carefully all His commandments and His statutes which I command you today, that all these curses will come upon you and overtake you: Cursed shall you be in the city, and cursed shall you be in the country. Cursed shall be your basket and your kneading bowl. Cursed shall be the fruit of your body and the produce of your land, the increase of your cattle and the offspring of your flocks. Cursed shall you be when you come in, and cursed shall you be when you go out. The Lord will send on you cursing, confusion, and rebuke in all that you set your hand to do, until you are destroyed and until you perish quickly, because of the wickedness of your doings in which you have forsaken Me. The Lord will make the plague cling to you until He has consumed you from the land which you are going to possess. The Lord will strike you with consumption, with fever, with inflammation, with severe burning fever, with the sword, with scorching, and with mildew; they shall pursue you until you perish. And your heavens which are over your head shall be bronze, and the earth which is under you shall be iron. The Lord will change the rain of your land to powder and dust; from the heaven it shall come down on you until you are destroyed. The Lord will cause you to be defeated before your enemies; you shall go out one way against them and flee seven ways before them; and you shall become troublesome to all the kingdoms of the earth. Your carcasses shall be food for all the birds of the air and the beasts of the earth, and no one shall frighten them away. The LORD will strike you with the boils of Egypt, with tumors, with the scab, and with the itch, from which you cannot be healed. The LORD will strike you with madness and blindness and confusion of heart. And you shall grope at noonday, as a blind man gropes in darkness; you shall not prosper in your ways; you shall be only oppressed and plundered continually, and no one shall save you. You shall betroth a wife, but another man shall lie with her; you shall build a house, but you shall not dwell in it; you shall plant a vineyard, but shall not gather its grapes. Your ox shall be slaughtered before your eyes, but you shall not eat of it; your donkey shall be violently taken away from before you, and shall not be restored to you; your sheep shall be given to your enemies, and you shall have no one to rescue them. Your sons and your daughters shall be given to another people, and your eyes shall look and fail with longing for them all day long; and there shall be no strength in your hand. A nation whom you have not known shall eat the fruit of your land and the produce of your labor, and you shall be only oppressed and crushed continually. So you shall be driven mad because of the sight which your eyes see. The LORD will strike you in the knees and on the legs with severe boils which cannot be healed, and from the sole of your foot to the top of your head. The LORD will bring you and the king whom you set over you to a nation which neither you nor your fathers have known, and there you shall serve other gods—wood and stone. And you shall become an astonishment, a proverb, and a byword among all nations where the LORD will drive you. You shall carry much seed out to the field but gather little in, for the locust shall consume it. You shall plant vineyards and tend them, but you shall neither drink of the wine nor gather the grapes; for the worms shall eat them. You shall have olive trees throughout all your territory, but you shall not anoint yourself with the oil; for your olives shall drop off. You shall beget sons and daughters, but they shall not be yours; for they shall go into captivity. Locusts shall consume all your trees and the produce of your land. The alien who is among you shall rise higher and higher above you, and you shall come down lower and lower. He shall lend to you, but you shall not lend to him; he shall be the head, and you shall be the tail. Moreover all these curses shall come upon you and pursue and overtake you, until you are destroyed, because you did not obey the voice of the LORD your God, to keep His commandments and His statutes which He commanded you. And they shall be upon you for a sign and a wonder, and on your descendants forever. Because you did not serve the LORD your God with joy and gladness of heart, for the abundance of everything, therefore you shall serve your enemies, whom the LORD will send against you, in hunger, in thirst, in nakedness, and in need of everything; and He will put a yoke of iron on your neck until He has destroyed you. The LORD will bring a nation against you from afar, from the end of the earth, as swift as the eagle flies, a nation whose language you will not understand, a nation of fierce countenance, which does not respect the elderly nor show favor to the young. And they shall eat the increase of your livestock and the produce of your land, until you are destroyed; they shall not leave you grain or new wine or oil, or the increase of your cattle or the offspring of your flocks, until they have destroyed you. They shall besiege you at all your gates until your high and fortified walls, in which you trust, come down throughout all your land;

and they shall besiege you at all your gates throughout all your land which the LORD your God has given you. You shall eat the fruit of your own body, the flesh of your sons and your daughters whom the LORD your God has given you, in the siege and desperate straits in which your enemy shall distress you. The sensitive and very refined man among you will be hostile toward his brother, toward the wife of his bosom, and toward the rest of his children whom he leaves behind, so that he will not give any of them the flesh of his children whom he will eat, because he has nothing left in the siege and desperate straits in which your enemy shall distress you at all your gates. The tender and delicate woman among you, who would not venture to set the sole of her foot on the ground because of her delicateness and sensitivity, will refuse to the husband of her bosom, and to her son and her daughter, her placenta which comes out from between her feet and her children whom she bears; for she will eat them secretly for lack of everything in the siege and desperate straits in which your enemy shall distress you at all your gates. If you do not carefully observe all the words of this law that are written in this book, that you may fear this glorious and awesome name, THE LORD YOUR GOD, then the LORD will bring upon you and your descendants extraordinary plagues—great and prolonged plagues—and serious and prolonged sicknesses. Moreover He will bring back on you all the diseases of Egypt, of which you were afraid, and they shall cling to you. Also every sickness and every plague, which is not written in this Book of the Law, will the LORD bring upon you until you are destroyed. You shall be left few in number, whereas you were as the stars of heaven in multitude, because you would not obey the voice of the LORD your God. And it shall be, that just as the LORD rejoiced over you to do you good and multiply you, so the LORD will rejoice over you to destroy you and bring you to nothing; and you shall be plucked from off the land which you go to possess. Then the LORD will scatter you among all peoples, from one end of the earth to the other, and there you shall serve other gods, which neither you nor your fathers have known— wood and stone. And among those nations you shall find no rest, nor shall the sole of your foot have a resting place; but there the LORD will give you a trembling heart, failing eyes, and anguish of soul. Your life shall hang in doubt before you; you shall fear day and night, and have no assurance of life. In the morning you shall say, 'Oh, that it were evening!' And at evening you shall say, 'Oh, that it were morning!' because of the fear which terrifies your heart, and because of the sight which your eyes see. And the LORD will take you back to Egypt in ships, by the way of which I said to you, 'You shall never see it again.' And there you shall be offered for sale to your enemies as male and female slaves, but no one will buy you."

~ PRAYER ~

Father, thank You for the clarity of Your Word. You have made it abundantly clear that You want me healthy and that as Your covenant child no sickness can befall me to overtake me. Jesus has redeemed me from the curse of the law. He has eradicated every one of these curses from my life. Your Word is clear, Father. I am blessed! Sickness has no right to reign in my life. In Jesus name, I am free!

——— *DECLARATION OF FAITH* ———

I am redeemed from the curse of the law. (Galatians 3:13.) I do not have to tolerate the curses of the covenant, for I am in Jesus and am firmly established in His righteousness. (Galatians 3:16.) I will not allow any of the curses of the Law to come upon me and overtake me.

I am redeemed from confusion and rebuke in the enterprises I undertake.

I am redeemed from destruction and shall not perish before my time. I am blessed to live a long, full, and satisfying life. (Psalm 91:16.)

I am redeemed from all pestilence which brings agonizing death.

I am redeemed from tuberculosis, cancer, and the progressive wasting of the body.

I am redeemed from fever.

I am redeemed from inflammation.

I am redeemed from the effects of drought.

I am redeemed from blight and decay.

I am redeemed from mildew.

I am redeemed from the sun scorching my garden.

I am redeemed from the ground choking my roots.

I am redeemed from powdery soil and dust.

I am redeemed from being defeated by my enemies.

I am redeemed from the fear of my enemies.

I am redeemed from boils.

I am redeemed from tumors.

I am redeemed from malignant diseases, which cause a discharge.

I am redeemed from scurvy (bleeding gums and livid skin patches).

I am redeemed from scabies, hives, rashes, and all skin diseases which cause an itch.

I am redeemed from madness (insanity). I have a sound mind and keep a clear head in every situation.

I am redeemed from blindness.

I am redeemed from confusion and the unsettling of the mind.

I am redeemed from indecision for lack of direction.

I am redeemed from being robbed.

I am redeemed from others sleeping with my spouse.

I am redeemed from others taking (stealing or confiscating) from me what I have built for myself.

I am redeemed from others gathering and taking (stealing or confiscating) my harvest from me. I have sown my seed and I will reap an abundant harvest.

I am redeemed from my animals being taken from me.

I am redeemed from my transportation being repossessed.

I am redeemed from my belongings being taken from me and given to my enemies.

I am redeemed from my sons and daughters being taken from me and given to another people. My hands are given power to prevent this.

I am redeemed from strangers consuming the fruit of my labor.

I am redeemed from being oppressed and crushed continually.

I am redeemed from being driven crazy by the things that I see.

I am redeemed from both leprosy and elephantiasis.

I am redeemed from infirmities of the knees and the legs.

I am redeemed from permanent runny sores that cannot be healed.

I am redeemed from being brought into slavery and forced to serve other gods.

I am redeemed from being jeered at for lack of blessing in my life.

I am redeemed from the worm eating the produce of my vine.

I am redeemed from sowing much seed, but gathering little harvest because the locusts [demons] have devoured it. All evil forces are bound and rebuked by the Lord! They cannot consume, steal, or restrain my harvest in any way! (Malachi 3:11.)

I am redeemed from having much, but not having the oil of anointing. My wealth is covered by the burden-removing, yoke-destroying power of God. Therefore, the abundance of my possessions cannot bring me anxiety in any shape or form.

I am redeemed from having my sons and daughters go into captivity.

I am redeemed from having locusts possess all of my trees, the fruit of my ground, and the products of my labor [my paycheck].

I am redeemed from having a stranger to the covenant and promises mount up higher and higher above me, while I go down lower and lower.

I am redeemed from having to borrow, which would make me the tail and not the head.

I am redeemed from having curses pursue me, come upon me and overtake me until I am destroyed.

I am redeemed from being a sign and a warning to other people of what it is like to be cursed because I chose to reject the abundance of God's blessings.

I am redeemed from having to serve my enemies.

I am redeemed from hunger and thirst.

I am redeemed from lack of clothing and being in want of all good things.

I am redeemed from having a yoke of iron around my neck until I am destroyed.

I am redeemed from being overcome by ruthless people.

I am redeemed from being besieged by a ruthless and powerful enemy.

I am redeemed from such severe famine that my only food would be my own sons and daughters.

I am redeemed from the strife that is caused by having all of my belongings taken from me.

I am redeemed from every sickness and plague that has a long duration.

I am redeemed from every disease that is brought upon the world.

I am redeemed from known sicknesses and unknown sicknesses.

I am redeemed from every sickness that has ever been or ever will be.

I am redeemed from being evicted from my land.

I am redeemed from myself and my loved ones being scattered and sent into slavery.

I am redeemed from having no rest from my labors.

I am redeemed from exhaustion in my heart [literally], my eyes, my mind, and my spirit.

I am redeemed from having my life hang in doubt so that I do not know what the future holds for me.

I am redeemed from being worried and having no assurance of what will take place in my life.

I am redeemed from hating life because of anxiety and dread due to the curses of the covenant.

I am redeemed from being sold again into slavery and hated so much that people see me as not even being worthy of bondage.

I am redeemed from all of this! None of it may come upon my life! I am in Christ Jesus and He has set me free!

(Hebrews 9:11,12; Isaiah 40:2; 52:13-53:12; John 8:32-36; 10:10; Exodus 15:26; Deuteronomy 7:15; Psalm 103)

DEUTERONOMY 30:14-20

"But the word is very near you, in your mouth and in your heart, that you may do it. See, I have set before you today life and good, death and evil, in that I command you today to love the LORD your God, to walk in His ways, and to keep His commandments, His statutes, and His judgments, that you may live and multiply; and the LORD your God will bless you in the land which you go to possess. But if your heart turns away so that you do not hear, and are drawn away, and worship other gods and serve them, I announce to you today that you shall surely perish; you shall not prolong your days in the land which you cross over the Jordan to go in and possess. I call heaven and earth as witnesses today against you, that I have set before you life and death, blessing and cursing; therefore choose life, that both you and your descendants may live; that you may love the LORD your God, that you may obey His voice, and that you may cling to Him, for He is your life and the length of your days; and that you may dwell in the land which the LORD swore to your fathers, to Abraham, Isaac, and Jacob, to give them."

~ *PRAYER* ~

I love You, Father. You are my life and the length of my days. All that I am and all that I have are found in You. All that I need or desire is in You. I stand in awe at the wonder of Your love. I need never fear sickness or disease again. You are always there with me and indeed You are within me. You have given me Your Word to heal me of all ailments. Your grace toward me is immeasurable. Your Word is in my mouth and in my heart. Call the witnesses together, Father, and I will boldly speak it. May all know that this day I choose life! I choose healing! I choose blessing! I will live and not die. I will multiply and increase in every way. I cling to my heavenly Father. I wrap my hands in Your garments and I will never let you go.

———— *DECLARATION OF FAITH* ————

The Word of faith is in my mouth continually. I keep it near to me—in my mouth, in my mind, and in my spirit—so that I may do and have what I say.

The Lord has set before me life and good things, but also death and evil things. The choice is mine. I choose to adhere to the statutes of His covenant. I walk in all of His ways so that I may live His abundant life and multiply in this earth.

Because I have chosen life, my Father is very pleased to bless me with His divine favor, good fortune, happiness, prosperity, and good things of every kind.

(Romans 10:8-10; Deuteronomy 11:26,27; Joshua 24:15; Psalms 35:27; 112:1-3)

CHAPTER FIVE

1 KINGS

1 KINGS 8:33-40 (ALSO IN 2 CHRONICLES 6:26-31)

"When Your people Israel are defeated before an enemy because they have sinned against You, and when they turn back to You and confess Your name, and pray and make supplication to You in this temple, then hear in heaven, and forgive the sin of Your people Israel, and bring them back to the land which You gave to their fathers. When the heavens are shut up and there is no rain because they have sinned against You, when they pray toward this place and confess Your name, and turn from their sin because You afflict them, then hear in heaven, and forgive the sin of Your servants, Your people Israel, that You may teach them the good way in which they should walk; and send rain on Your land which You have given to Your people as an inheritance. When there is famine in the land, pestilence or blight or mildew, locusts or grasshoppers; when their enemy besieges them in the land of their cities; whatever plague or whatever sickness there is; whatever prayer, whatever supplication is made by anyone, or by all Your people Israel, when each one knows the plague of his own heart, and spreads out his hands toward this temple: then hear in heaven Your dwelling place, and forgive, and act, and give to everyone according to all his ways, whose heart You know (for You alone know the hearts of all the sons of men), that they may fear You all the days that they live in the land which You gave to our fathers."

~ PRAYER ~

Father, You are merciful and gracious. You do not see me through the stain of sin, but through the eyes of grace. You had Jesus become the atoning sacrifice for our sins. Through His shed blood, the power of sin is broken and I have been set free. Therefore, Father, I will not let my past hinder me any longer. Teach me the good way in which to walk. When the enemy besieges me with his foul sicknesses and diseases, remember our covenant, Father. I am Your born-again son/daughter and heir to Your kingdom. In Jesus I live and move and have my being. As I spread my hands to You and speak Your Word, cause Your healing power to flow through every fiber of my being.

———— DECLARATION OF FAITH ————

My Lord Jesus defeated Satan and all demons at the cross. The power of sin has been broken and I have been set free. I have power over all of the power of the enemy and nothing shall by any means harm me. I know that the good way is the way of health and prosperity. I walk in the good way and remain healthy all the days of my life. I stand strong through famine, blight, mildew, germs, locusts, and grasshoppers. When the enemy besieges me to destroy me with sickness and disease, I remain strong. The Lord has stationed Himself within

*me and He is greater than all. He hears my every prayer and delivers
me with mighty acts of judgment every single time.*

(Colossians 1:13,14; 2:11-15; Romans 6:14; Luke 10:19; 3 John 2; 1 John 4:4;
Ephesians 6:10-18)

1 KINGS 17:17-24

Now it happened after these things that the son of the woman who
owned the house became sick. And his sickness was so serious that
there was no breath left in him. So she said to Elijah, "What have I to
do with you, O man of God? Have you come to me to bring my sin
to remembrance, and to kill my son?" And he said to her, "Give me
your son." So he took him out of her arms and carried him to the
upper room where he was staying, and laid him on his own bed.
Then he cried out to the LORD and said, "O LORD my God, have You
also brought tragedy on the widow with whom I lodge, by killing her
son?" And he stretched himself out on the child three times, and
cried out to the LORD and said, "O LORD my God, I pray, let this
child's soul come back to him." Then the LORD heard the voice of
Elijah; and the soul of the child came back to him, and he revived.
And Elijah took the child and brought him down from the upper
room into the house, and gave him to his mother. And Elijah said,
"See, your son lives!" Then the woman said to Elijah, "Now by this I
know that you are a man of God, and that the word of the LORD in
your mouth is the truth."

~ PRAYER ~

Father, You alone are God. There is no other. Stretch forth Your hand to do wonders on behalf of Your Son Jesus. For He condemned sin in the flesh and set free those held captive by it. He is the Lord of my life and the propitiation that guarantees my healing. Sin is no longer an issue. It cannot hold back Your healing power from my life. I know that with You it is never too late to pray for complete recovery. Stretch forth Your hand, Father. Confirm Your Word with signs following.

——— DECLARATION OF FAITH ———

No matter how serious the sickness, it is no match for the healing power of my God. Even if the very breath within me has failed and I am seconds away from death, I can be healed. Furthermore, nothing but my own lack of faith can hold God's healing power from me. If I falter, I need only to call for the elders of the church to anoint me with oil and pray for me. I have the unfailing Word that the prayer of faith shall save the sick and the Lord shall raise them up. Therefore, no matter what the circumstances show, I can be healed!

(James 5:14,15; Mark 16:18-20; Romans 8:3)

CHAPTER SIX

2 KINGS

2 KINGS 5:1-14

Now Naaman, commander of the army of the king of Syria, was a great and honorable man in the eyes of his master, because by him the LORD had given victory to Syria. He was also a mighty man of valor, but a leper. And the Syrians had gone out on raids, and had brought back captive a young girl from the land of Israel. She waited on Naaman's wife. Then she said to her mistress, "If only my master were with the prophet who is in Samaria! For he would heal him of his leprosy." And Naaman went in and told his master, saying, "Thus and thus said the girl who is from the land of Israel." Then the king of Syria said, "Go now, and I will send a letter to the king of Israel." So he departed and took with him ten talents of silver, six thousand shekels of gold, and ten changes of clothing. Then he brought the letter to the king of Israel, which said, Now be advised, when this letter comes to you, that I have sent Naaman my servant to you, that you may heal him of his leprosy. And it happened, when the king of Israel read the letter, that he tore his clothes and said, "Am I God, to kill and make alive, that this man sends a man to me to heal him of his leprosy? Therefore please consider, and see how he seeks a quarrel with me." So it was, when Elisha the man of God heard that the king of Israel had torn his clothes, that he sent to the king, saying, "Why have you torn your clothes? Please let him come to me, and he shall know that there is a prophet in Israel." Then Naaman went with his horses and chariot, and he stood at the door of Elisha's house. And Elisha sent a messenger to him, saying, "Go and wash in the Jordan seven times, and your flesh shall be restored to you, and you shall be clean." But Naaman became furious, and went away and said, "Indeed, I said to myself, 'He will surely come out to me, and stand and call on the name of the LORD his God, and wave his hand over the place, and heal the leprosy.' Are not the Abanah and the Pharpar, the rivers of Damascus, better than all the waters of Israel? Could I not wash in them and be clean?" So he turned and went away in a rage. And his servants came near and spoke to him, and said, "My father, if the prophet had told you to do something great, would you not have done it? How much more then, when he says to you, 'Wash, and be clean'?" So he went down and dipped seven times in the Jordan, according to the saying of the man of God; and his flesh was restored like the flesh of a little child, and he was clean.

~ *PRAYER* ~

Father, I humble myself under Your mighty hand that You may exalt me in due time. I do not look to my own position to earn me any points to bring forth my healing. My trust is in You and You alone. I will gladly do whatever You require. I am obedient to Your Word, for it is the only avenue to my complete deliverance and recovery.

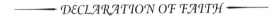
—— *DECLARATION OF FAITH* ——

I am not offended by the requirements of the Lord and His prophets. Whatever the Lord requires of me, I am obedient to perform. Therefore, I arise cleansed of my infirmities. Sickness and disease cannot cling to me, for I have done what the Lord requires and He has declared that I am healed.

(2 Chronicles 20:20; Deuteronomy 28:1; John 14:15; Isaiah 53:4,5; Psalm 103:1-5; Exodus 15:26; James 5:14-16)

2 Kings 20:1–6 (also in Isaiah 38:1-5)

In those days Hezekiah was sick and near death. And Isaiah the prophet, the son of Amoz, went to him and said to him, "Thus says the LORD: 'Set your house in order, for you shall die, and not live.'" Then he turned his face toward the wall, and prayed to the LORD, saying, "Remember now, O LORD, I pray, how I have walked before You in truth and with a loyal heart, and have done what was good in Your sight." And Hezekiah wept bitterly. And it happened, before Isaiah had gone out into the middle court, that the word of the LORD came to him, saying, "Return and tell Hezekiah the leader of My people, 'Thus says the LORD, the God of David your father: "I have heard your prayer, I have seen your tears; surely I will heal you. On the third day you shall go up to the house of the LORD. And I will add to your days fifteen years. I will deliver you and this city from the hand of the king of Assyria; and I will defend this city for My own sake, and for the sake of My servant David.'"

~ PRAYER ~

Father, You are good and Your mercy endures forever. You are always with me to reveal when sickness and disease have come to destroy me. But I refuse to fear, Father. I know You. You are kind and gracious. Abundant life is found in You and You alone. Therefore, I turn my face aside from all distractions and focus on Your promise. Heal me according to Your unfailing Word, Father. Redeem my life from destruction. Turn the evil report into a glorious one. Fulfill the number of my years that I may fulfill the calling that You have on my life.

DECLARATION OF FAITH

I refuse to lay claim to an evil report. Any and every report that contradicts the Word of my God I consider to be false and misleading.

I know the power of God that is at work within me. He is faithful and what He has spoken will come to pass in my life.

Therefore, when the evil report comes, I set my face to the wall. I do not look upon, nor listen to, that which is contrary to the Word. I will accept nothing less than what God has promised.

I lay claim to my inheritance as God's son/daughter. Peace, joy, healing, and prosperity belong to me. I need only to remind my Father of these things and He changes the bad report to good.

(Philippians 4:6-9; Ephesians 1:3,11,17-23; Isaiah 43:26; 55:11; Psalm 56:1-11; Numbers 14:5-9)

CHAPTER SEVEN

2 CHRONICLES

2 CHRONICLES 7:14-16

If My people who are called by My name will humble themselves, and pray and seek My face, and turn from their wicked ways, then I will hear from heaven, and will forgive their sin and heal their land. Now My eyes will be open and My ears attentive to prayer made in this place. For now I have chosen and sanctified this house, that My name may be there forever; and My eyes and My heart will be there perpetually.

~ PRAYER ~

Father, remember that You have chosen me as Your dwelling place in this earth. Your name is upon me forever. Your eyes and Your heart are with me perpetually. Give ear to my petitions, Lord. Take sickness from me as You have promised. Teach me the laws of healthy living. Reveal to me every wicked way that robs me of Your divine health so that I may turn and live the life that You have called me to live.

——— *DECLARATION OF FAITH* ———

The land that I dwell on is subject to my dominion.

When I humble myself and seek the face of my Father, He hears from heaven and brings healing to the land.

His ears are ever opened to my prayers and His eye never leaves me.

He has chosen me and set me apart as an ambassador of the kingdom.

He has placed His name upon me, and His eyes and heart are with me both now and forevermore.

(Psalm 8:6; Ephesians 1:22; James 4:10; 1 John 5:14,15; 2 Corinthians 5:17-21; Genesis 12:1-3)

2 CHRONICLES 30:13-20

Now many people, a very great assembly, gathered at Jerusalem to keep the Feast of Unleavened Bread in the second month. They arose and took away the altars that were in Jerusalem, and they took away all the incense altars and cast them into the Brook Kidron. Then they slaughtered the Passover lambs on the fourteenth day of the second month. The priests and the Levites were ashamed, and sanctified themselves, and brought the burnt offerings to the house of the LORD. They stood in their place according to their custom, according to the Law of Moses the man of God; the priests sprinkled the blood received from the hand of the Levites. For there were many in the assembly who had not sanctified themselves; therefore the Levites had charge of the slaughter of the Passover lambs for everyone who was not clean, to sanctify them to the LORD. For a multitude of the people, many from Ephraim, Manasseh, Issachar, and Zebulun, had not cleansed themselves, yet they ate the Passover contrary to what was written. But Hezekiah prayed for them, saying, "May the good LORD provide atonement for everyone who prepares his heart to seek God, the LORD God of his fathers, though he is not cleansed according to the purification of the sanctuary." And the LORD listened to Hezekiah and healed the people.

~ PRAYER ~

Father, I do not take for granted this wonderful grace that I enjoy. Jesus has cleansed me and made me whole. Sin cannot destroy me or cause You to turn away from me. You have heard my cry and have answered my prayer. I am healed from the top of my head to the bottom of my feet.

—— DECLARATION OF FAITH ——

Though I have sinned horribly in His sight, my Father has forgiven me. I sought Him with all of my heart and He heard my cry for mercy. Though I was unclean, He pardoned me. Though I was undeserving, He placed His loving hands upon me and healed me.

(Psalms 18:1-19; 103:1-12; 2 Chronicles 19:3; Romans 3:21-26; Ephesians 2:1-10)

CHAPTER EIGHT

PSALMS

PSALM 6:1-10

O LORD, do not rebuke me in Your anger, Nor chasten me in Your hot displeasure. Have mercy on me, O LORD, for I am weak; O LORD, heal me, for my bones are troubled. My soul also is greatly troubled; but You, O LORD—how long? Return, O LORD, deliver me! Oh, save me for Your mercies' sake! For in death there is no remembrance of You; in the grave who will give You thanks? I am weary with my groaning; all night I make my bed swim; I drench my couch with my tears. My eye wastes away because of grief; it grows old because of all my enemies. Depart from me, all you workers of iniquity; for the LORD has heard the voice of my weeping. The LORD has heard my supplication; the LORD will receive my prayer. Let all my enemies be ashamed and greatly troubled; let them turn back and be ashamed suddenly.

~ PRAYER ~

Father, I thank You that Your anger has been taken from me. I no longer need to fear Your wrath. You do not rebuke me in anger or chasten me in hot displeasure. You now see me as clean through the blood of Jesus. You are not the cause of my sicknesses. You are not Jehovah-flu or Jehovah-cancer. You are Jehovah Rapha—the God who heals me. You have healed my troubled bones and have delivered my soul from all anxiety. I find my dwelling between Your shoulders and rest in Your mercy and grace. Fever must flee from me as I lift my hands in honor of Your name. You give me joy in place of mourning and gladness supplants my grief. Devils of sickness must take flight. All that they have brought upon me is returned to their own heads.

——— *DECLARATION OF FAITH* ———

The Lord has heard my supplication and has risen in my defense. All of my enemies shall be defeated before my face. They have met with the fierce anger of my Father and run from me utterly terrified. Sudden disaster has come upon them and they shall not escape.

(Exodus 15:26; Deuteronomy 2:25; 2 Chronicles 20:15-25; Psalms 7:16; 103:3; 140:9; Esther 9:25; James 4:7)

PSALM 13:3-6

Consider and hear me, O LORD my God; enlighten my eyes, lest I sleep the sleep of death; lest my enemy say, "I have prevailed against him"; lest those who trouble me rejoice when I am moved. But I have trusted in Your mercy; my heart shall rejoice in Your salvation. I will sing to the LORD, because He has dealt bountifully with me.

~ *PRAYER* ~

Father, enlighten the eyes of my understanding that I may become familiar with the exceeding greatness of Your healing power within me. Let not the enemy say that he has prevailed over me. I align myself with Your Word, Father. I stand in agreement with it and boldly declare that I shall live and not die! I trust in Your mercy and rejoice in Your salvation. I sing praises to Your name, for You are worthy. You deal bountifully with me and never hold back Your good gifts. I expect nothing but good things from You both now and forevermore.

———— *DECLARATION OF FAITH* ————

The Lord considers my ways and hears me when I pray. He enlightens my eyes, lest I sleep the sleep of death. My enemies shall have no cause to rejoice over me. I remain strong and ready. The joy of the Lord is my strength. His Word to me is unfailing. I will sing to the Lord and bless His holy name, for He has dealt bountifully with me. No matter what my circumstances show, I know that I am healed by the stripes of Jesus!

(Ephesians 1:3,17-23; Isaiah 53:3-5; Psalms 21:3,4; 34:8-10; 103:1-5; 107:20,21)

PSALM 16:5-9

O LORD, You are the portion of my inheritance and my cup; You maintain my lot. The lines have fallen to me in pleasant places; yes, I have a good inheritance. I will bless the LORD who has given me counsel;

my heart also instructs me in the night seasons. I have set the LORD always before me; because He is at my right hand I shall not be moved. Therefore my heart is glad, and my glory rejoices; my flesh also will rest in hope.

~ PRAYER ~

Father, every good and perfect gift comes from You. You have never once given me an evil report. You always fill my cup with goodness and my inheritance in You is full of wonderful treasures. I have tasted of Your counsel and have found You to be good. You hold me close to Your heart and keep me from all harm. You even speak to my heart when I sleep, and when I awake I find You at my side. Because You are at my right hand, I shall not be moved. Sickness and disease cannot cling to me. Heartache and sorrow must flee. At the mere thought of You, my heart is glad and my glory rejoices. My flesh also shall rest in hope, for You make it Your business to bring me healing in every way.

—— DECLARATION OF FAITH ——

My heavenly Father has assigned me my share of His inheritance and my cup overflows continually. He has set my boundaries in a spacious and pleasant land and has given me a delightful endowment.

I praise the Lord for His counsel. Even at night, my spirit guides me in His way. With Him at my right hand, I shall stand strong in every circumstance.

What a joy it is to be a child of God! My heart leaps within me and my tongue rejoices in His praise! I am raised with Jesus and shall never be abandoned to hell. He has made known to me the path of life and fills me with joy in His presence. At His right hand, I shall have abundant pleasures for all of eternity.

(Romans 6:3-5; 8:14-17; Ephesians 1:3,4; 2:6; 6:10; Psalms 23:5; 139:24; Acts 2:22-39; John 16:13)

PSALM 21:2-4

You have given him his heart's desire, and have not withheld the request of his lips. Selah. For You meet him with the blessings of goodness; You set a crown of pure gold upon his head. He asked life from You, and You gave it to him—length of days forever and ever.

~ PRAYER ~

You are so good to me, Father. I marvel at the thought of how much You love me. You give me my heart's desire and never withhold my requests. You always meet me with blessings of goodness. You set a crown of pure gold upon my head. I ask for healing and You freely give it. I ask for life and You give it to me abundantly. Under Your hedge of protection, I shall live a long, full, and satisfying life.

——— DECLARATION OF FAITH ———

I rejoice in the strength of my Father, for He has given me my heart's desire. He who knows me better than I know myself has prepared the way for me and has given me an inheritance to perfectly suit my needs and personality. All of my requests are granted and my joy knows no bounds!

A crown of pure gold has been placed upon my head and abundance rains down on me like a satisfying spring rain.

I asked life of Him and He gave it to me. The length of my days is now eternal! Forever I will praise His name!

My glory abounds in His salvation. Honor and majesty have been placed upon me. I am now born again under the bloodline of the King!

My Father's glory surrounds me and His presence is within me. I trust in Him and I am not afraid. Because of His mercy, I shall not be moved.

(John 16:23,24; Psalm 79:12; Genesis 12:1-3; Exodus 23:27; James 4:7; Isaiah 41:10-13; Deuteronomy 32:30; Ephesians 6:10-18)

PSALM 27:13,14

I would have lost heart, unless I had believed that I would see the goodness of the LORD in the land of the living. Wait on the LORD; be of good courage, and He shall strengthen your heart; wait, I say, on the LORD!

~ PRAYER ~

Father, Your Word is so full of love towards me. Such knowledge is beyond imagination. How can I respond to such compassion? How can I honor You but believe in what You have said? Father, if no one else will take You at Your Word, I will. All that You do for me is for good, and all that You ask of me is that I receive it by faith. I choose to believe, Lord. I refuse to be afraid. Strengthen my heart in accordance with Your Word. Show me Your goodness in the land of the living.

——— *DECLARATION OF FAITH* ———

I remain steadfast and confident in the fact that I will see the goodness of God in my life. I will be strong and take heart for I know that He is with me. I will wait for His manifestation of power. I will be patient and wait upon the Lord.

(Deuteronomy 6:24; Psalm 23:6; Ephesians 6:10; Isaiah 40:29-31)

PSALM 30:1-5

I will extol You, O LORD, for You have lifted me up, and have not let my foes rejoice over me. O LORD my God, I cried out to You, and You healed me. O LORD, You brought my soul up from the grave; You have kept me alive, that I should not go down to the pit. Sing praise to the LORD, you saints of His, and give thanks at the remembrance of His holy name. For His anger is but for a moment, His favor is for life; weeping may endure for a night, but joy comes in the morning.

~ *PRAYER* ~

Father, I praise You for You are worthy. I extol You, for You have lifted me up. You do not allow my enemies to rejoice over me. You have heard my cry and healed me of my ailments. In You I find life and length of days worth living. Thank You, Father, for Your wonderful grace. I live in the comfort of Your boundless favor. I may weep for a night, but joy comes in the morning. I may suffer for a moment, but my deliverance never fails.

———— *DECLARATION OF FAITH* ————

When the enemy comes against my body, I will take my refuge in the Lord. When I call to Him, He heals me. He delivers me from the clutches of the grave and spares me from the consequences of hell and the curse.

I will sing His praises with a sincere and upright heart, for He has given me an intimate knowledge of His ways and His will.

His anger lasts only a moment, but His favor and abundance of blessings last a lifetime.

I may weep during the night, but He will raise me up with rejoicing in the morning.

The Lord loves me and favors me as His own son/daughter. He makes me to stand firm so that I will never be shaken. The stronghold that I have built is saturated with His anointing. I cannot be defeated or overrun.

(Psalms 97:12; 103:1-18; 2 Peter 2:24; Galatians 3:13; 1 Corinthians 2:6-16; Isaiah 26:20; 54:7)

Psalm 34:17-19

The righteous cry out, and the LORD hears, and delivers them out of all their troubles. The LORD is near to those who have a broken heart, and saves such as have a contrite spirit. Many are the afflictions of the righteous, but the LORD delivers him out of them all.

~ PRAYER ~

Father, I know that You hear my every prayer as I humble myself before You. You never fail to answer and honor Your Word on my behalf. The enemy rains down his afflictions, but You deliver me out of every one! Consider my situation, Father. Liberate me from the hardship that I face. Heal my broken heart and rescue my life from destruction. Strengthen me in the power of Your might that I may continue to advance Your kingdom to the praise of Your mighty name.

—— DECLARATION OF FAITH ——

I love and enjoy the life that God has given me. All of my days are good ones, for I have chosen to live the God-kind of life. I have made my unyielding decision to keep my tongue from speaking evil things and to tell the truth in every situation. I have turned from the ways of the wicked and have focused my attention firmly on doing only that which is good.

I do not let peace escape from my life. I seek it like a relentless hunter and capture it as a precious prize.

The eyes of my Father never leave me and His ear is always opened to my prayers.

Though troubles come against me on a regular basis, the Lord delivers me out of every one!

My Father comforts me when I am brokenhearted. When my spirit is crushed and I feel all alone, He wraps His tender arms around me and embraces me in His love.

I am faced with troubles of many kinds, but the Lord delivers me out of every one.

(Acts 17:28; Psalms 51:17; 145:18,19; Proverbs 24:16; Genesis 12:1-3; Romans 8:1; 14:19; 1 Peter 3:10-12; James 1:26; John 10:10; Isaiah 1:16,17; Amos 9:4)

PSALM 38:3-22

There is no soundness in my flesh because of Your anger, nor any health in my bones because of my sin. For my iniquities have gone over my head; like a heavy burden they are too heavy for me. My wounds are foul and festering because of my foolishness. I am troubled, I am bowed down greatly; I go mourning all the day long. For my loins are full of inflammation, and there is no soundness in my flesh. I am feeble and severely broken; I groan because of the turmoil of my heart. Lord, all my desire is before You; and my sighing is not hidden from You. My heart pants, my strength fails me; as for the light of my eyes, it also has gone from me. My loved ones and my friends stand aloof from my plague, and my relatives stand afar off. Those also who seek my life lay snares for me; those who seek my hurt speak of destruction, and plan deception all the day long. But I, like a deaf man, do not hear; and I am like a mute who does not open his mouth. Thus I am like a man who does not hear, and in whose mouth is no response. For in

You, O LORD, I hope; You will hear, O Lord my God. For I said, "Hear me, lest they rejoice over me, lest, when my foot slips, they exalt themselves against me." For I am ready to fall, and my sorrow is continually before me. For I will declare my iniquity; I will be in anguish over my sin. But my enemies are vigorous, and they are strong; and those who hate me wrongfully have multiplied. Those also who render evil for good, they are my adversaries, because I follow what is good. Do not forsake me, O LORD; O my God, be not far from me! Make haste to help me, O Lord, my salvation!

~ PRAYER ~

Father, I thank You that I live in the day of Your grace. You have forgiven my every sin and redeemed my life from destruction. You prepare a table of blessing for me in the presence of my enemies. You give me power over all of their power and declare that nothing shall by any means harm me. None of the devil's sicknesses can prosper over me. None of his diseases can overtake me. You are near to me, Father, in all of Your strength and majesty! Therefore, I know that my circumstances shall change. Those who seek my hurt shall see me strong in the Lord and in the power of His might. Do you hear me, Satan? In Jesus' name, I bind your every act against me and loose the Lord's healing power into my life. I shall not say that I am sick; I say that I am healed!

——— DECLARATION OF FAITH ———

My Father is faithful to deliver me from every evil attack. He gives me strength to overcome, that I may tread on the enemy's high places.

By the Lord's anointing, I overcome every burden and destroy every yoke of oppression. Inflammation and foul, festering wounds are healed from my body. I replace sorrow and grief with the sound of mighty praise! Anguish is turned to joy and my strength is renewed as my enemies look on in terror.

(Luke 10:17-20; Ephesians 6:10; Isaiah 10:27; 61:1-3; Exodus 15:26)

PSALM 41:1–3

Blessed is he who considers the poor; the LORD will deliver him in time of trouble. The LORD will preserve him and keep him alive, and he will be blessed on the earth; You will not deliver him to the will of his enemies. The LORD will strengthen him on his bed of illness; You will sustain him on his sickbed.

~ PRAYER ~

Father, I thank You for Your spiritual laws of reciprocity. When I come to the aid of others, You come to mine. You build your hedge of protection around me as I give to Your cause. You preserve me and keep me alive. You make Your declaration to all of heaven that I am to be blessed and You rescue me from the will of my enemies. You sustain and strengthen me when sickness attacks. I cannot be defeated, for I live under the commanded blessing of almighty God.

—— DECLARATION OF FAITH ——

I am a shield to those who lack the strength to stand against the devil's evil schemes. I am a comfort to the needy and a provider for the poor. Because of this, the Lord delivers me out of every trouble and distressing situation.

He preserves my life from the attacks of the enemy and blesses me with His favor and abundance. He sustains me when sickness comes to take me from His work, and He restores me to my true, energetic, and healthy self.

(Psalms 5:11,12; 27:12; 103:1-5; 112:1-3; Isaiah 40:29-31; James 5:14-16)

PSALM 73:26

My flesh and my heart fail; but God is the strength of my heart and my portion forever.

~ *PRAYER* ~

Father, I thank You that I am not confined to the healing power in this natural world. I am not limited to worldly resources. My flesh and heart may fail, but You are my strength and my portion forever. By Your power, Father, I am healed and kept alive.

DECLARATION OF FAITH

I am always with the Lord—He holds me by my right hand. He guides me continually with His counsel as I walk the many paths of this life, and He will stay with me until the day I am taken up to be with Him in glory. This earth has nothing that I desire outside of Him.

Though flesh and heart fail, God is my strength and my portion forever. He alone is my glory and the sustainer of my life.

(John 16:13; Psalms 16:5; 32:8; 48:14; 84:2; Isaiah 58:11; Philippians 3:8)

PSALM 79:11

Let the groaning of the prisoner come before You; according to the greatness of Your power preserve those who are appointed to die.

~ PRAYER ~

Father, I thank You that You hear my prayers. I trust in the greatness of Your power to deliver me from any and every distressing situation. Even if I am given up to die, You preserve me. My health shall be restored and I will live out my days in a full and abundant life.

——— DECLARATION OF FAITH ———

The Lord hears my every prayer and executes judgment on my behalf. He fills me full of His healing power. When all earthly hope is gone and I've been given up to die, He preserves my life. The bondage of sickness cannot hold me down. I am free in Christ Jesus!

(Philippians 2:25-27; John 10:10; Ephesians 1:17-23)

PSALM 91

He who dwells in the secret place of the Most High shall abide under the shadow of the Almighty. I will say of the LORD, "*He is* my refuge and my fortress; my God, in Him I will trust." Surely He shall deliver you from the snare of the fowler and from the perilous pestilence. He shall cover you with His feathers, and under His wings you shall take refuge; His truth *shall be your* shield and buckler. You shall not be afraid of the terror by night, nor of the arrow *that* flies by day, nor of the Pestilence that walks in darkness, nor of the destruction that lays waste at noonday. A thousand may fall at your side, and ten thousand at your right hand; but it shall not come near you. Only with your eyes shall you look, and see the reward of the wicked. Because you have made the LORD, who is my refuge, even the Most High, your dwelling place, no evil shall befall you, nor shall any plague come near your dwelling; for He shall give His angels charge over you, to keep you in all your ways. In their hands they shall bear you up, lest you dash your foot against a stone. You shall tread upon the lion and the cobra, the young lion and the serpent you shall trample underfoot. "Because he has set his love upon Me, therefore I will deliver him; I will set him on high, because he has known My name. He shall call upon Me, and I will answer him; I will be with him in trouble; I will deliver him and honor him. With long life I will satisfy him, and show him My salvation."

~ PRAYER ~

Father, I dwell in Your secret place and abide under Your shadow. You are my refuge and my fortress—my God, and in You I do trust. I draw near to You with all that I am. My dwelling place is between Your shoulders. You have delivered me from Satan's snares and You shield me from his deadly diseases. You cover me with Your feathers and under Your wings I take refuge. Your Word is my shield and defense. I am not afraid of the terror of the night, nor the arrow that flies by day, nor the pestilence that stalks the darkness, nor the destruction that lays waste at noonday. A thousand may fall at my side and ten thousand at my right hand, but it shall not come near me. You are my Father and I have made You my refuge. Therefore, no evil can befall me and no plague can come near my dwelling. You have given Your angels charge over me to keep me in all of my ways. They bear me up in their hands lest I dash my foot against a stone. In You I have authority over all of the authority of the enemy. I tread upon the lion and the cobra; the young lion and the serpent I trample under my feet. Because I have set my love upon You, You deliver me. You set me on high because I know Your name. When I call upon You, You answer me. You are with me in times of trouble, and You never fail to deliver me. You even set me in a place of honor in the presence of all. I am humbled at the thought of such love. I am held secure in Your tender embrace. I am shielded in Your hedge of protection. You satisfy me with long life and show me Your salvation. You are so good, Father. I am Yours forever.

——— DECLARATION OF FAITH ———

I dwell in the secret place of the Most High and rest, remaining steadfast and secure, under the shadow of the Almighty. He is my refuge and my fortress, my God and Father, and I trust Him with all of my heart.

He has given me a sure and certain deliverance from the traps of Satan and has freed me from all deadly pestilence.

He has covered me with His feathers and under His wings I have taken refuge. His faithfulness is my shield and my rampart.

I do not fear the terror of the night, nor the arrow that flies by day, nor the pestilence that stalks in the darkness, nor the plague that lays waste at noonday. A thousand may fall at my side, even ten thousand at my right hand, but it shall not come near me.

I will see with my own eyes the punishment of the wicked.

The Most High God, my heavenly Father, is my fortress and my habitation.

He has accepted me as His own. I am a son/daughter in His royal family.

Therefore, no evil may befall me, and no plague, sickness, or disaster is allowed to come near my dwelling.

God has commanded the angels to set up camp around me as sentinels in my life. They guard me in all of my ways and keep me from all harm. They bear me up in their hands lest I dash my foot against a stone.

I tread upon the lion and the cobra. The young lion and the serpent, I trample under my feet. The devil's power over me has been completely stripped away. God has made a decree (a fixed law) concerning me, saying, "I will rescue him/her from every calamity; I will protect him/her because he/she acknowledges My name. He/She will call upon Me and I will answer him/her. I will be with him/her in times of trouble. I will deliver him/her and set him/her in the place of

highest honor. With long life I will satisfy him/her and show him/her
My salvation."

(Psalms 9:10; 17:8; 27:5; 34:7; 37:34; 90:1; 112:7; 124:7; 142:5; Isaiah 25:4;
32:2; 43:1,2; 46:4; Proverbs 6:5; 12:21; Job 1:10; 5:19; 2 Timothy 1:7;
1 John 5:18; Malachi 1:5; Matthew 4:6; 26:53; Hebrews 1:14;
Exodus 23:20-23; 2 Kings 6:15-17; Luke 4:10,11; 10:19; Ephesians 2:6)

PSALM 92:12-15

The righteous shall flourish like a palm tree, he shall grow like a cedar in Lebanon. Those who are planted in the house of the LORD shall flourish in the courts of our God. They shall still bear fruit in old age; they shall be fresh and flourishing, to declare that the LORD is upright; He is my rock, and there is no unrighteousness in Him.

~ PRAYER ~

Father, it is abundantly obvious that sickness, disease, and disaster are not from You. You are my Rock and there is no unrighteousness in You. You cause me to flourish like the palm tree and grow like the cedar in Lebanon. You plant me in Your house and I prosper in Your courts. You cause me to bear fruit even in old age. No matter what my circumstances are, I remain full of life. I thrive like a green leaf. You keep me healthy, wealthy, and wise so that I may continue to declare that You are upright. You are not the cause of calamity. You are my healer and deliverer—my glory and the lifter of my head.

I flourish in this earth like the palm tree. Though the winds blow with hurricane force, I remain fixed, steadfast, and secure.

I am planted in the very house of almighty God, and I grow like the cedar of Lebanon.

Under God's care, I thrive at the height of success and development. I continue to bear good fruit throughout my life and even in old age I remain fresh and green, with a shout of victory on my lips proclaiming, "The Lord is faithful and to be honored! He is my Rock and no wicked way can be found in Him!"

(Psalms 1:1-3; 3:3; Matthew 7:24,25; Joshua 1:8; Jeremiah 29:11; 1 Corinthians 10:4)

PSALM 103:1-5

Bless the LORD, O my soul; and all that is within me, bless His holy name! Bless the LORD, O my soul, and forget not all His benefits: Who forgives all your iniquities, Who heals all your diseases, Who redeems your life from destruction, Who crowns you with lovingkindness and tender mercies, Who satisfies your mouth with good things, so that your youth is renewed like the eagle's.

~ PRAYER ~

Father, I truly bless You with all that is within me. I exalt and magnify Your holy name. You are God and there is no other. You daily load me with Your benefits. You have forgiven all of my sins and healed all of my diseases. You redeem my life from destruction. You crown me with lovingkindness and tender mercies. You satisfy my mouth with good things so that my youth is renewed like the eagle's. You are good to me, Father. Your embrace lifts my spirit to praise Your holy name!

──────── DECLARATION OF FAITH ────────

I stir up my inner man to praise the name of the Lord. My soul and all that is within me shall praise Him.

I will not forget all that God has done for me, all that He has for me, and all that He is doing in my life.

He has forgiven me of all of my sins and healed me of every possible disease.

He has redeemed my life from the pit and has crowned me with His love and compassion.

He satisfies my every desire with good things so that my youth is renewed like the eagle's.

(Ephesians 3:16; Deuteronomy 7:9; 8:6-18; 2 Timothy 1:6; Galatians 3:13; Isaiah 40:7,31; 53:4,5; 54:17; Exodus 15:26; 34:6,7)

PSALM 107:17-22

Fools, because of their transgression, and because of their iniquities, were afflicted. Their soul abhorred all manner of food, and they drew near to the gates of death. Then they cried out to the LORD in their trouble, and He saved them out of their distresses. He sent His word and healed them, and delivered them from their destructions. Oh, that men would give thanks to the LORD for His goodness, and for His wonderful works to the children of men! Let them sacrifice the sacrifices of thanksgiving, and declare His works with rejoicing.

~ PRAYER ~

Thank You, Father, for revealing to me that there is more to living in divine health than just praying for healing. Open my eyes to know what foods I should eat and what foods to avoid. Show me what supplements I should take in order to feed my body properly and keep it healthy. I repent of unhealthy living, Father. Save me from my distresses and give me a new start. I receive the healing power in Your Word and set myself in agreement with it. I am delivered from destruction! Thank You for Your goodness to me, Father. You are so kind and loving. You forgive my wrong doing and wipe the slate clean. I am so elated by Your fellowship. Knowing You fills me with joy unspeakable and full of glory. I shall declare Your works with rejoicing. What a pleasure it is to be a child of almighty God!

——— DECLARATION OF FAITH ———

I am not so foolish as to think that I can live in divine health regardless of how I treat my body. I purpose in my heart to feed it properly and give it the rest and exercise it needs to remain at optimum performance.

However, I do not have to live by natural means alone. God has sent His Word into this earth to heal me and rescue me from death. His love for me never fails. He is always working to bring good things into my life and perform mighty deeds on my behalf.

(Matthew 8:8; 2 Kings 20:5; Isaiah 53:4,5; Psalm 30:2; Proverbs 3:3,4; Job 33:28-30)

PSALM 118:16,17

The right hand of the LORD is exalted; the right hand of the LORD does valiantly. I shall not die, but live, and declare the works of the LORD.

~ PRAYER ~

Thank You, Father, for revelation knowledge of Your Word. Your right hand, Jesus, is exalted! He has done valiantly. In Him I shall live and not die. Satan cannot steal my testimony. I shall declare Your works, Father, and give glory to Your name.

──── DECLARATION OF FAITH ────

I have the complete and unqualified certainty that victory is mine.

I would much rather take my refuge in the Lord than to trust in the ways of men. Even the princes of this earth are paupers compared to the ones who are in alliance with God.

All I need to do is lift up the name of Jesus in my defense and they are thwarted.

Even when I stumble in battle, the Lord lifts me up. He is always with me and He never stumbles. He is my strength, my song, and my

*continual salvation. Shouts of victory are constantly heard in my house,
for the Lord is a mighty God and has done great things on my behalf!*

(Ephesians 2:1-10; John 3:16,17; Colossians 1:13,14; Hebrews 13:5,6;
1 Corinthians 15:57; Romans 8:31; 12:9-21; 2 Timothy 1:7; 2:13;
Genesis 12:3; 2 Chronicles 32:7; 2 Kings 6:15-17; Psalms 35:4; 54:4;
59:10; 88:17; 146:3)

PSALM 119:65–68

You have dealt well with Your servant, O LORD, according to Your
Word. Teach me good judgment and knowledge, for I believe Your
commandments. Before I was afflicted I went astray, but now I keep
Your Word. You are good, and do good; teach me Your statutes.

~ PRAYER ~

Father, You deal well with me according to Your Word. I choose to
believe it without wavering. No matter what the circumstances show,
I will continue steadfast in faith. Teach me good judgment and knowledge, Father. Give me revelation of Your precepts. I know You are
good and what You do is good. You do not send evil things such as
sickness and disease in order to instruct me. I am taught according to
Your Word, and Your Word declares that I am healed. I choose to
believe Your Word over religious misconceptions, and I will walk in it
as a good son/daughter should.

——— *DECLARATION OF FAITH* ———

I am taught by the best. God, the very Creator of heaven and earth, is my master instructor.

He delivered me from a life full of turmoil and has shown me the way to live in His peace.

His goodness to me is revealed in His Word. By it, I have learned to retain knowledge and good judgment. God is good and everything that He does for me is good.

With Him as my teacher, I am gaining extensive understanding of His ways and how I am to incorporate them into my life.

(Psalm 33:5; John 16:13; 2 Corinthians 5:17; Romans 14:17; Daniel 1:17,20; 2:22,23; Genesis 50:20; 1 Corinthians 2:6-16)

PSALM 128:1-6

Blessed is every one who fears the LORD, who walks in His ways. When you eat the labor of your hands, you shall be happy, and it shall be well with you. Your wife shall be like a fruitful vine in the very heart of your house, your children like olive plants all around your table. Behold, thus shall the man be blessed who fears the LORD. The LORD bless you out of Zion, and may you see the good of Jerusalem all the days of your life. Yes, may you see your children's children. Peace be upon Israel!

~ PRAYER ~

Father, I tremble at the thought of Your majesty. You are my life and my salvation. You alone sustain me and cause me to draw breath. You are the center of all my trust. You always know what is best; therefore, I will always do what You tell me to do. Because of You, I eat the labor of my hands in happiness. Because of You, it goes well with me and my children after me. Because of You, my spouse is productive and my children are like olive plants around my table. Health and happiness are mainstays in my household. Peace and security surround me like a fortress. Favor covers me like a shield. You do bless me with good things of every kind, Father. All the days of my life I will enjoy Your goodness and mercy. I will see my children grow and enjoy the blessing of grandchildren. This is Your Word to me, Father, and I believe it with all of my heart.

——— DECLARATION OF FAITH ———

I walk in the ways of almighty God as a good son/daughter and disciple. I mimic His ways. In every way possible, I live like God lives.

I eat the fruit of my labor and live my life in happiness, peace, divine favor, and good fortune of every kind.

My wife/husband is fruitful and productive within my house, and my children are anointed and blessed at my table.

My life is a pleasure to live.

(Ephesians 5:1; John 10:10; Ecclesiastes 2:24; 3:22; Psalms 5:11,12; 52:8; 144:12; 127:3-5; Proverbs 31:10-31; 1 Peter 3:10,11)

PSALM 146:5-8

Happy is he who has the God of Jacob for his help, whose hope is in the LORD his God, Who made heaven and earth, the sea, and all that is in them; Who keeps truth forever, Who executes justice for the oppressed, Who gives food to the hungry. The LORD gives freedom to the prisoners. The LORD opens the eyes of the blind; the LORD raises those who are bowed down; the LORD loves the righteous.

~ PRAYER ~

Father, in You I have confident expectation of good things. You are my never failing help in time of need. You keep truth forever and execute justice when I am oppressed. You always meet my every need no matter what my circumstances are. You raise me up when I'm bowed down. You lift my head and give me revelation of who I am in Christ Jesus. You give food to the hungry, open the eyes of the blind, and set the captives free. What a joy it is to know that I'm Your child forever. Your love for me is unshakable and You delight in fulfilling Your Word on my behalf. I am saved, delivered, and healed. Nothing shall by any means harm me. I am free!

—— DECLARATION OF FAITH ——

The Lord has set me free from the chains of oppression.

He has given me all that I need.

He has healed my eyes and lifted my head.

I am His own special child and He loves me with all of His heart.

(Isaiah 61:1-3; Philippians 4:11-19; Psalm 3:3; Romans 8:14-17,38,39)

PSALM 147:1-3

Praise the LORD! For it is good to sing praises to our God; for it is pleasant, and praise is beautiful. The LORD builds up Jerusalem; He gathers together the outcasts of Israel. He heals the brokenhearted and binds up their wounds.

~ PRAYER ~

Father, You are the God of all comfort who comforts His children in times of tribulation. You heal my broken heart and bind up my wounds. No matter what I face, You are there with me to guide me through it. I will praise You in the midst of the turmoil, Father. I praise You and exalt Your mighty name! You are the God who heals. You lift my head in Your hands and strengthen me so that I may advance Your kingdom to the praise of Your glory.

—— DECLARATION OF FAITH ——

It is good to sing praises to God in the midst of trying circumstances. No matter what my situation, I will praise Him, for He gathers me under His wings and heals my broken heart. He binds up my wounds and heals me from head to toe. He strengthens me in every way so that I may do His will without hindrance or interruption.

(2 Corinthians 1:3,4; Psalms 34:15-20; 91:3-10; Proverbs 4:11-13; Exodus 15:26)

CHAPTER NINE
PROVERBS

PROVERBS 2:10,11

When wisdom enters your heart, and knowledge is pleasant to your soul, discretion will preserve you; understanding will keep you.

~ PRAYER ~

Thank You, Father, for giving me wisdom and understanding. I have Your blessing of wisdom and revelation for healthy living. Your knowledge is pleasant to my soul and I receive it without dispute. I know that my Father knows best. Therefore, I will let discretion preserve me and understanding keep me. With Your wisdom, Father, I prosper and remain in good health, even as my soul prospers.

—— DECLARATION OF FAITH ——

The Lord guides me on a path of justice and preserves my way before me. I understand righteousness, justice, equity, and every good path. Wisdom finds its home in my heart and knowledge is pleasant to my soul. Discretion preserves me and understanding protects me. I have within me all the wisdom that I need to live a healthy and prosperous life.

(Psalm 25:19-21; Proverbs 11:4,5; Ephesians 1:17,18; 3 John 2)

PROVERBS 3:1,2,7,8

My son, do not forget my law, but let your heart keep my commands; for length of days and long life and peace they will add to you... Do not be wise in your own eyes; fear the LORD and depart from evil. It will be health to your flesh, and strength to your bones.

~ *PRAYER* ~

Father, I know that Your commands bring me length of days, long life, and peace. I don't give my attention to how I feel or what the situation looks like. I do not lend credence to doctors' reports or any negative testimony the enemy brings my way. I know the truth is found in You, Father. My trust is in You and You alone. I have Your Word that if I live according to Your precepts and trust You with unwavering confidence, that if I turn away from those things that poison my body and focus on that which is good and right, You will bring health to all of my flesh and strength to all of my bones.

—— *DECLARATION OF FAITH* ——

I do not forget the benefits of living wisely.

I understand the rules that I must follow in order to be a success in life and I submit to them willingly. Because of this, my life is prolonged by many years and my prosperity overflows like a geyser in a desert land.

I shun all evil and look to God for my provision. This brings health and vitality to my body and strength to all of my bones.

(Psalms 1:1-3; 91:16; 103:1-5; Joshua 1:8; Deuteronomy 6:5-7; 28:1-14; Isaiah 46:4; Romans 8:11; 12:16)

PROVERBS 3:13-18

Happy is the man who finds wisdom, and the man who gains understanding; for her proceeds are better than the profits of silver, and her gain than fine gold. She is more precious than rubies, and all the things you may desire cannot compare with her. Length of days is in her right hand, in her left hand riches and honor. Her ways are ways of pleasantness, and all her paths are peace. She is a tree of life to those who take hold of her, and happy are all who retain her.

~ *PRAYER* ~

Father, I am so thankful that Jesus has become my wisdom, my righteousness, my sanctification, and my redemption. I have found true wisdom and it has made me a happy man/woman. Through Jesus, I live my life in pleasantness and steadfast security. I stand in agreement with Your Word, Father. Length of days, long life, and peace are now mine. I am saved, delivered and healed from the top of my head to the bottom of my feet!

——— *DECLARATION OF FAITH* ———

I am a healthy and prosperous man/woman, full of wisdom and understanding.

I know the profits and returns of knowledge. I pursue her with a whole heart. It is a great joy to me when I find her. She is more precious to me than any treasure on the face of the earth. Long life is in her right hand and in her left are riches and honor. I have determined to embrace her like a lover. My union with her brings me happiness, prosperity, and health.

I shall enjoy the pleasantries of life, follow the paths of peace, and end my days an old, vibrant, and happy man/woman.

(Psalms 119:34-38,65-68; 1 John 1:3; 2:27; 1 Corinthians 2:6-16; Job 28:13; Matthew 11:29; 13:44; 1 Timothy 4:8)

PROVERBS 4:20-27

My son, give attention to my words; incline your ear to my sayings. Do not let them depart from your eyes; keep them in the midst of your heart; for they are life to those who find them, and health to all their flesh. Keep your heart with all diligence, for out of it spring the issues of life. Put away from you a deceitful mouth, and put perverse lips far from you. Let your eyes look straight ahead, and your eyelids look right before you. Ponder the path of your feet, and let all your ways be established. Do not turn to the right or the left; remove your foot from evil.

~ *PRAYER* ~

Father, Your Word is the foundation of all that I do. I give my complete attention to what You have to say about my situation. I will not give ear to an evil report. Your Word is unchangeable truth. I hold it above all pomp and circumstance. I will not let it depart from my eyes, for it is life to me and health to all of my flesh. I keep my heart with all diligence, Father. I reject all influence that is contrary to Your Word. I fill my heart with Your truth and out of the abundance of my heart my mouth speaks. I will not cancel my blessings by speaking doubt and unbelief. I ponder the path of my feet, and my ways are established in Your Word. I will never turn away from it by believing the devil's lies. I remove my foot from evil and set my feet on the path of victory, in Jesus' name!

——— *DECLARATION OF FAITH* ———

The path the Lord has laid before me is as a shining light that shines more and more unto a perfect day.

I attend to the words of the Lord and incline my ear to His sayings. I do not let them depart from my eyes but keep them in the midst of my heart; for the Word is life to me and it brings health to all of my flesh.

Above all else, I diligently guard my heart, for it is the wellspring of my life.

I do not speak perverse, obstinate, or wicked talk. Negative and corrupt language does not come out of my mouth.

My eyes look straight ahead. They are fixed on the prize set before me.

I achieve my goals without distraction or wavering. I deliberate and premeditate over every step that I take. I will only move forward in ways that are stable and well established.

I cannot be lured into the ways of Satan.

I follow the ways of the Lord.

(Psalms 1:1-3; 107:20; 119:105; 1 Corinthians 9:24; 2 Corinthians 2:11; Proverbs 5:21; Ephesians 5:1-21; Deuteronomy 6:6-9; 28:1)

PROVERBS 10:11

The mouth of the righteous is a well of life.

~ *PRAYER* ~

Father, I thank You for Your Word that declares that I am now the righteousness of God in Christ Jesus my Lord. My mouth is a well of life. My words, Father, in agreement with Your precepts, bring health and healing to all who are touched by them.

——— DECLARATION OF FAITH ———

The words of my mouth are a reservoir—a fountain—the very source that brings into being both who I am and what I have.

(Proverbs 18:20,21; Mark 11:22-25; Matthew 17:20; 2 Corinthians 4:13; Hebrews 11:1)

PROVERBS 12:18

There is one who speaks like the piercings of a sword, but the tongue of the wise promotes health.

~ PRAYER ~

Father, I thank You for giving me the wisdom of Your Word. I do not speak like the piercings of a sword. My words bring health to the situation and life to all who hear them.

—— *DECLARATION OF FAITH* ——

I am a man/woman of understanding. I am wise in the methods of words. My tongue brings healing from every direction and in every form.

(1 Corinthians 2:6-16; Proverbs 18:20,21; Mark 11:22-25)

PROVERBS 13:3

He who guards his mouth preserves his life, but he who opens wide his lips shall have destruction.

~ PRAYER ~

Father, I thank You for revealing to me the power in the words that I speak. My very life is preserved when my words are in agreement with Yours. Therefore, I am determined to speak only those things which are pure and of a good report. Negative and destructive speech shall be far from my lips. I make my conversation harmonious with Your Word and live my life in health and happiness.

——— *DECLARATION OF FAITH* ———

By the words of my mouth, I obtain and enjoy all good things. I am careful not to speak those things that would strip me of my blessings. My words produce health, joy, love, peace, prosperity, and power in my life. My mouth is stubborn and inflexible. My words are good ones, and coupled with my diligence and hard work, all of my desires are fully satisfied.

(Mark 11:22-25; Proverbs 18:20,21; Deuteronomy 28:12)

PROVERBS 14:30

A sound heart is life to the body, but envy is rottenness to the bones.

~ *PRAYER* ~

Father, You have made my heart to pump life into my body. Therefore, I will do what it takes to keep it sound and working properly.

You have revealed to me that my beliefs, attitudes, and emotions can have either a positive or negative effect on my health. Therefore, I choose to bring healing to my life through love, affection, and unwavering faith. I will not allow envy, strife, and evil speaking to fill my body full of rottenness and deadly poisons.

——— *DECLARATION OF FAITH* ———

I am a patient and self-controlled man/woman with a deep under-standing of the ways of life.

My spirit is at peace within me, and it gives health and vitality to my body.

(Galatians 5:22,23; Romans 8:11; 14:17; Proverbs 16:32; James 1:19)

PROVERBS 15:4

A wholesome tongue is a tree of life, but perverseness in it breaks the spirit.

~ *PRAYER* ~

Father, I wrap my hands in Your garments and keep You close to me at all times. Train me to speak the right things so that my words are a tree of life. Keep me from perverseness and negative words that would break my spirit and fill my world with death and destruction.

——— *DECLARATION OF FAITH* ———

My words bring healing to all who are touched by them. They are a tree of life, with limbs branching out and roots spreading within, forming an impregnable fortress of God's glory in this earth.

(Proverbs 18:20,21; Mark 11:22-25; Psalm 107:20)

PROVERBS 15:30

The light of the eyes rejoices the heart, and a good report makes the bones healthy.

~ PRAYER ~

Father, just knowing that You love me brings a smile to my face. In You, my eyes reflect sheer joy and steadfast confidence. Your report of me has been spoken and cannot be changed. I am healed by the stripes of Jesus!

──── DECLARATION OF FAITH ────

I am a man/woman of many smiles and a cheerful countenance. I am known to bring a good report. When I speak, health and vitality flow into the bones of those who hear.

(Philippians 4:4; Nehemiah 8:10; Numbers 14:8; Psalm 107:20)

PROVERBS 16:24,25

Pleasant words are like a honeycomb, sweetness to the soul and health to the bones. There is a way that seems right to a man, but its end is the way of death.

~ PRAYER ~

Father, You make it so clear to me how powerful my words truly are. I will not be as a son/daughter who doesn't listen. I hear and obey. I know how to order my manner of speech. My words are pleasant words. They are like a honeycomb that brings sweetness to my soul and health to my bones. I choose not to listen to the so-called common sense of society. They may think they have it right, but they do not know You. Their ways are the ways of death, but Your ways, Father, are life and peace.

——— *DECLARATION OF FAITH* ———

My words are pleasant words. They are as a honeycomb, sweet to the mind and healing to the bones.

(Proverbs 15:1,4,30; 18:20,21; Psalm 107:20)

PROVERBS 17:22

A merry heart does good, like medicine, but a broken spirit dries the bones.

~ *PRAYER* ~

Father, when I consider all of the good things You have done for me, I find no reason to be unhappy. I rejoice in Your presence. I will not allow my spirit to be broken through negative emotions and destructive beliefs. My merry heart does good like a medicine, and the joy You have given me fills me with courage and strength every day of my life.

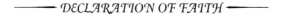

———— *DECLARATION OF FAITH* ————

I have a cheerful, happy, and positively joyful heart, which sends its healing power to every fiber of my being!

(Philippians 4:4; Nehemiah 8:10; Proverbs 12:25; Romans 8:11)

PROVERBS 18:14

The spirit of a man will sustain him in sickness, but who can bear a broken spirit?

~ *PRAYER* ~

Father, Your promises give me such a positive outlook. In You, I find no reason to despair. You richly provide all the healing power I need to live a happy and blessed life.

———— *DECLARATION OF FAITH* ————

My spirit is powerful and full of joy. It sustains me when sickness wages war against my body.

(Ephesians 3:16; Romans 8:11; Nehemiah 8:10)

PROVERBS 18:20,21

A man's stomach shall be satisfied from the fruit of his mouth; from the produce of his lips he shall be filled. Death and life are in the power of the tongue, and those who love it will eat its fruit.

~ *PRAYER* ~

Father, I love Your Word and the principles contained therein. I love that You have given me power to have the things that I say. I am thrilled by the fact that my healing springs forth speedily as I align my words with Your perfect will. I commit myself to speak words of life. Therefore, I declare in faith that I am a healthy and happy man/woman!

———— *DECLARATION OF FAITH* ————

My words produce the fruit that fills my stomach, and my lips produce the harvest by which I am satisfied. The elements of life and death yield themselves to the power of my tongue. My words are seeds of life and prosperity to the kingdom of God, but death and destruction to the kingdom of the enemy. I sow my words wisely and reap a harvest that makes my Father proud.

(Proverbs 12:14; 13:2; Mark 11:22-25; Galatians 6:7-9)

CHAPTER TEN

ISAIAH

ISAIAH 6:10

"Make the heart of this people dull, and their ears heavy, and shut their eyes; lest they see with their eyes, and hear with their ears, and understand with their heart, and return and be healed."

~ PRAYER ~

Father, You have softened my heart and filled me with precious knowledge. Through Your anointing I clearly see the things that You have done for me. You are my Father, not my enemy. You are not my problem. You never cause pain and destruction to come upon me. I know beyond all shadow of doubt that You are my healer. I rest in Your powerful embrace.

———— DECLARATION OF FAITH ————

My heart is not dull and my ears are not heavy. I fully understand that my God is Jehovah Rapha, the Lord my healer. He is not Jehovah

Cancer. He is not Jehovah Disease. He is not Jehovah Pain. He is Jehovah Rapha, the Lord who heals me.

(Ephesians 4:18; Exodus 15:26; Isaiah 53:3-5)

ISAIAH 19:21,22

Then the LORD will be known to Egypt, and the Egyptians will know the LORD in that day, and will make sacrifice and offering; yes, they will make a vow to the LORD and perform it. And the LORD will strike Egypt, He will strike and heal it; they will return to the LORD, and He will be entreated by them and heal them.

~ PRAYER ~

Father, You speak of Egypt as a type of the world and its godless system. Therefore, I know by this Word that healing is mine. I have come to You and You have accepted me as Your own. I know that You take care of Your own. You saw my need and met it in full. I am healed and that's all there is to it.

—— DECLARATION OF FAITH ——

I have revelation knowledge of all that Jesus did for me. In Him, I have complete healing in every area of my life. I was in a wretched condition, but He sought me out, and found me. When I cried out for forgiveness, He heard me and healed all of my diseases.

(Matthew 8:17; Exodus 15:26; Psalm 38:3-22)

ISAIAH 33:24

The inhabitant will not say, "I am sick"; the people who dwell in it will be forgiven their iniquity.

~ *PRAYER* ~

Father, I set myself in agreement with Your Word. You have forgiven all of my sins and healed all of my diseases. I will not say, "I am sick," for that is contrary to what You have accomplished in me. I will trust in Your Word and say with utter certainty, "I am healed."

───── *DECLARATION OF FAITH* ─────

I understand the power of the spoken word. I refuse to say, "I am sick."[1] To the contrary, I am redeemed! I am filled with health, energy, and vitality! All of my sins have been forgiven, and I enjoy the blessings that my new covenant with God has provided!

(Psalms 91:9,10; 103:2,3; Galatians 3:13; Proverbs 18:20,21)

ISAIAH 35:1-6

The wilderness and the wasteland shall be glad for them, and the desert shall rejoice and blossom as the rose; it shall blossom abundantly and rejoice, even with joy and singing. The glory of Lebanon shall be given to it, the excellence of Carmel and Sharon. They shall see the glory of the LORD, the excellency of our God. Strengthen the weak hands, and make firm the feeble knees. Say to those who are fearful-hearted, "Be strong, do not fear! Behold, your God will come with vengeance, with the recompense of God; He will come and save you." Then the eyes of the blind shall be opened, and the ears of the deaf shall be unstopped. Then the lame shall leap like a deer, and the tongue of the dumb sing. For waters shall burst forth in the wilderness, and streams in the desert.

~ PRAYER ~

Father, I praise Your holy name. You have caused such goodness to flood my life. In all that I do, I blossom and rejoice. I break forth with singing and joy fills my soul. I shall see Your glory: the excellency of my God. Strengthen my hands, Father. Speak Your blessing over me. Cause Your Word to ring true in my life. Father, I say in agreement with Your Word that I am strong in Jesus. I have no fear for You have come with a vengeance. You heal blind eyes and unstop deaf ears. The lame leap like a deer and the mute tongue sings Your praises. You cause waters to burst forth in my wilderness places and streams to flow on my barren lands. You are awesome to behold. You have said it, and you make good on it. All praise to Your holy name!

—— DECLARATION OF FAITH ——

I give strength to those with feeble hands and hold steady those whose knees are giving way. I am a steadfast source of encouragement to those who are afraid of an evil report. I say to those who are terrified, "Be strong and take courage, for God is on your side! He loves you and will come to your aid with a vengeance and with divine retribution. He will not forsake you. Because of His great love for you, He will deliver you."

Because of this, the eyes of the blind are opened, the ears of the deaf are unstopped, the lame leap like a deer, the mute tongue shouts for joy, water gushes forth in the midst of a wilderness, and nourishment flows into a desert land. The burning sand has become like a pool and the cracked earth is fed with springs of fresh water. Where devils once ran rampant, God's blessings now flow.

A highway called the way of holiness is with me, and those who love the Word flock to it. Satan and his hordes look upon it and flee in stark terror, for we who walk in the way are redeemed and translated into a new kingdom. We enter that kingdom with singing, and everlasting joy crowns our heads. Happiness and joy overtake us and sorrow and sighing flee away.

(Psalm 18:3-19; Colossians 1:10-14; Deuteronomy 3:28; Isaiah 35:8; Mark 16:15-18)

ISAIAH 41:10

"'Fear not, for I am with you; be not dismayed, for I am your God. I will strengthen you, yes, I will help you, I will uphold you with My righteous right hand.'"

~ *PRAYER* ~

Father, what have I to fear when I have Your promise that You will never leave me? You are always with me. You strengthen me when I feel weak and help me whenever I am in need. You always uphold me with Your righteous right hand. You draw me close to Your chest and set my dwelling between Your shoulders. I am not afraid, Father. I rest in the shadow of Your wings.

I have no cause for fear, for my God is with me. I will not be dismayed, for God is my Father and He has promised to never leave me nor forsake me. He strengthens me and assists me in every circumstance. He upholds me with His righteous right hand so that my victory is made certain.

(Joshua 1:5-9; Nehemiah 8:10; Psalms 3; 91:14-16)

ISAIAH 42:5-7

Thus says God the LORD, Who created the heavens and stretched them out, Who spread forth the earth and that which comes from it, Who gives breath to the people on it, and spirit to those who walk on it: "I, the LORD, have called you in righteousness, and will hold your hand; I will keep you and give you as a covenant to the people, as a light to the Gentiles, to open blind eyes, to bring out prisoners from the prison, those who sit in darkness from the prison house.

~ PRAYER ~

Father, I know that right now You are holding my hand. You are my Father and my God. You have called me in righteousness and made me Your covenant partner for all of eternity. No sickness or malady can cling to me as I walk in Your ways. You have turned me from darkness to stand in Your glorious light. From this day to eternity, I can expect nothing but good things from You. Thank You for Your compassion and unfailing help, Father. I bless Your holy name.

──────── *DECLARATION OF FAITH* ────────

I have a covenant with God sealed with the blood of the Messiah. In Him, I am made complete. He has taken hold of my hand so that I can have confidence in every step that I take. He has made me His own child and has accepted responsibility for me. He keeps me close to His heart and will never let me go.

Through my Lord, I open the eyes of the blind and set the captives free. Those bound by the chains of darkness are released in my presence, for God is in me and His glory shines through me. It is my Lord, the Anointed One and His anointing, who does these great and mighty works.

(John 10:34-38; 14:10-14; Hebrews 8:6-13; Acts 2:43; 4:30-33; 5:16; 6:8)

ISAIAH 46:3,4

"Listen to Me, O house of Jacob, and all the remnant of the house of Israel, who have been upheld by Me from birth, who have been carried from the womb: even to your old age, I am He, and even to gray hairs I will carry you! I have made, and I will bear; even I will carry, and will deliver you."

~ PRAYER ~

Father, even in old age I have Your blessing of healing to sustain me. You do not hold back Your healing because I am old. You still see me as Your precious child and Your promises will always apply to me. No matter what my circumstances are showing, You carry me and deliver me through them.

———— DECLARATION OF FAITH ————

I am the covenant partner of almighty God. He has upheld me from birth and He sustains me even in old age. He made me and will bear me. He will always carry me and deliver me from every trouble that I face.

(Psalms 18:1,2; 37:25; Deuteronomy 28:1-14; 32:9-12)

ISAIAH 53:1-6

Who has believed our report? And to whom has the arm of the LORD been revealed? For He shall grow up before Him as a tender plant, and as a root out of dry ground. He has no form or comeliness; and when we see Him, there is no beauty that we should desire Him. He is despised and rejected by men, a Man of sorrows and acquainted with grief. And we hid, as it were, our faces from Him; He was despised, and we did not esteem Him. Surely He has borne our griefs and carried our sorrows; yet we esteemed Him stricken, smitten by God, and afflicted. But He was wounded for our transgressions, He was bruised for our iniquities; the chastisement for our peace was upon Him, and by His stripes we are healed. All we like sheep have gone astray; We have turned, every one, to his own way; and the LORD has laid on Him the iniquity of us all.

~ PRAYER ~

Father, I have seen Your glorious arm and I have believed Your report. I believe that Jesus bore my sicknesses and carried my pains. He was wounded for my transgressions and bruised for my iniquities. The chastisement for my peace was upon Him, and with the stripes that wounded Him I am healed. Father, I know that it was an awesome and awful price that Jesus had to pay for me. He took all of Your wrath so that I could be healed. This is a great truth, Lord, and I choose to walk in it with unwavering confidence.

—— DECLARATION OF FAITH ——

Jesus bore my sicknesses and carried my pains. He was smitten, afflicted, and pierced through the hands and feet because of my transgressions. He was bruised and battered because of my wickedness. He became sick with my sicknesses and suffered excruciating pain on my account.

What He did on that cross and in those three days and nights of pain, He did willingly. He took my punishment upon Himself and gave me His peace in return. Because of His wounds, I am made well. I am now totally healed in spirit, soul, and body. In Him, I am made whole.

I was like a sheep that had turned to his own way and I rejected the way of righteousness, but the Lord laid all of my iniquities, first to last, upon Jesus and now there is nothing left that can separate me from Him.

(1 Peter 2:24; Colossians 2:10; Ephesians 2:14; Hebrews 10:14; Romans 8:38,39)

ISAIAH 55:11

So shall My word be that goes forth from My mouth; it shall not return to Me void, but it shall accomplish what I please, and it shall prosper in the thing for which I sent it.

~ *PRAYER* ~

Father, You said that You sent Your Word to heal me. Therefore, according to this promise that Word will not return void, but it will accomplish the task You sent it forth to do. You have declared my healing. Therefore I am healed, in Jesus' name!

——— *DECLARATION OF FAITH* ———

As rain and snow fall from heaven to water the earth and make it bring forth seed for the sower and bread for the eater, so it is with God's Word. He has sent it to me for a purpose and it will accomplish that purpose in my life. It is continually on my lips as a seed and it brings me a perpetual harvest of good things. What a joy it is to be led forth in such peace and assurance! The mountains and the hills burst forth into song before me and I enjoy the goodwill of all who see God's favor in my life.

(Isaiah 55:10; Mark 4:14-20; Psalms 107:20; 119:138-140; Proverbs 3:3,4; 2 Corinthians 9:10,11)

ISAIAH 57:15-19

For thus says the High and Lofty One Who inhabits eternity, whose name is Holy: "I dwell in the high and holy place, with him who has a contrite and humble spirit, to revive the spirit of the humble, and to revive the heart of the contrite ones. For I will not contend forever, nor will I always be angry; for the spirit would fail before Me, and the souls which I have made. For the iniquity of his covetousness I was angry and struck him; I hid and was angry, and he went on backsliding in the way of his heart. I have seen his ways, and will heal him; I will also lead him, and restore comforts to him and to his mourners. I create the fruit of the lips: Peace, peace to him who is far off and to him who is near," says the LORD, "And I will heal him."

~ PRAYER ~

Father, I have humbled myself under Your mighty hand. Therefore, I know that You dwell with me and are indeed within me. You revive my heart and restore me to perfect health and vitality. You do not chastise me with anger, nor do You use sickness to teach me. All of Your wrath was placed on Jesus so that all of Your love could be poured out upon me. You are always there to lead me in the truth. You restore comforts to me and cause me to live in peace and security. You take these words that I speak and create what I need from them. In You, Father, my healing is thoroughly guaranteed.

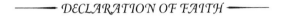

——— DECLARATION OF FAITH ———

My road has been built up and custom-made for me. All obstacles have been removed from my path.

I have been revived, made alive in the spirit, and regenerated as a brand-new creation, with God himself living in my heart.

God has declared to me that His anger has been removed. All of my sins and willful ways have been put behind me and I can now enter into His presence fearlessly, without the slightest sense of guilt for what I have done.

I am now under the gentle care of my heavenly Father. He heals, guides, and comforts me in my way. He has replaced my sorrow with shouts of praise. He has decreed that I am to live securely—in perfect peace, health, and safety. Healing is mine, and that is God's final Word on it.

(Psalm 27:11; Titus 3:5; Proverbs 4:18,26,27; Hebrews 4:16; James 5:15)

ISAIAH 58:6-11

"Is this not the fast that I have chosen: to loose the bonds of wickedness, to undo the heavy burdens, to let the oppressed go free, and that you break every yoke? Is it not to share your bread with the hungry, and that you bring to your house the poor who are cast out; when you see the naked, that you cover him, and not hide yourself from your own flesh? Then your light shall break forth like the morning, your healing shall spring forth speedily, and your righteousness shall go before you; the glory of the LORD shall be your rear guard. Then you shall call, and the LORD will answer; you shall cry, and He will say, 'Here I am.' If you take away the yoke from your midst, the pointing of the finger, and speaking wickedness, if you extend your soul to the hungry and satisfy the afflicted soul, then your light shall dawn in the darkness, and your darkness shall be as the noonday. The LORD will guide you continually, and satisfy your soul in drought, and strengthen your bones; you shall be like a watered garden, and like a spring of water, whose waters do not fail."

~ PRAYER ~

Father, I choose to fast for the right reasons. My purpose is to loose the bonds of wickedness and undo heavy burdens, so that the captive may go free. I know that sickness is a burden that the devil uses to hold people in bondage. I refuse to allow that in my life. My light shall break forth like the morning and my healing shall spring forth speedily. Father, You have made me the righteousness of God in Christ Jesus my Lord. That righteousness goes before me and Your glory, Father, is my rear guard. I now have the guarantee that You will answer my every prayer. You are always with me and You anoint me with burden-removing, yoke-destroying power. By Your power within me, I make light shine in the darkness and my darkness is as noonday. Father, You alone are my unfailing guide. You satisfy my soul in drought and strengthen all of my bones. I am like a watered garden, and like a spring, my waters do not fail.

——— *DECLARATION OF FAITH* ———

The fast that God has ordained for me is this: to set the captive free, to loose the chains of injustice, to break the yoke of oppression off of every neck, to share my food with the hungry, to provide the poor and homeless with shelter, to clothe the naked, and to take special care of those in my own household. By these, my radiance springs forth like the dawn and my healing comes to me quickly and without fail.

The righteous One goes before me and the glory of the Lord is my rear guard.

I call upon the Lord and He answers me. He entertains my every prayer.

The Lord guides me continually and satisfies my every need, even in a fruitless and sun-scorched land. He strengthens my frame and makes me like a well-watered garden—like a spring whose waters never fail.

(Psalms 1:1-3; 23; 34:7; 139:5; John 16:13; Philippians 4:11-13,19; Luke 4:18,19; Nehemiah 5:10-12; Exodus 14:19; Isaiah 61:1-3)

ISAIAH 61:1-3

"The Spirit of the Lord GOD is upon Me, because the LORD has anointed Me to preach good tidings to the poor; He has sent Me to heal the brokenhearted, to proclaim liberty to the captives, and the opening of the prison to those who are bound; to proclaim the acceptable year of the LORD, and the day of vengeance of our God; to comfort all who mourn, to console those who mourn in Zion, to give them beauty for ashes, the oil of joy for mourning, the garment of praise for the spirit of heaviness; that they may be called trees of righteousness, the planting of the LORD, that He may be glorified."

~ PRAYER ~

Father, in Jesus You have met all of my needs and more. I no longer have to bear the burdens of poverty and sickness. The anointing shatters those yokes, and I am now free to serve You in prosperity and health. You give me beauty for ashes and joy in place of mourning. I put on the garment of praise to counter the spirit of heaviness. I am a tree of righteousness—a planting of the Lord so that You, Father, may be glorified now and forevermore.

——— DECLARATION OF FAITH ———

The Holy Spirit is within me, and I have the burden-removing, yoke-destroying power to preach the gospel to the poor, heal the broken-hearted, set free those held captive by the devil, release the prisoners from their dungeon of darkness, proclaim to all that God is not mad at them and is ready to grant them abundant favor and blessings, to tell of the day of God's vengeance, comfort all who mourn, provide for those who grieve and present them with a crown of beauty in place of ashes, the oil of happiness instead of mourning, and a garment of praise to cure their depression. I am known as an oak of righteousness, a planting of the Lord to display His love and splendor to all the world.

(2 Corinthians 1:20-22; Mark 16:15-18; Job 29:12-17; 1 John 2:27)

CHAPTER ELEVEN

JEREMIAH

JEREMIAH 17:13-14

O LORD, the hope of Israel, all who forsake You shall be ashamed. "Those who depart from Me shall be written in the earth, because they have forsaken the LORD, the fountain of living waters." Heal me, O LORD, and I shall be healed; save me, and I shall be saved, for You are my praise.

~ PRAYER ~

Father, You are the heart of all of my praise. I worship and adore You. You have healed me, and I shall be healed. You have saved me, and I shall be saved. You are my fountain of living waters, and I will praise You forevermore.

My trust and focus are on the Lord alone. He has declared me to be healed; therefore, I am healed. He has declared my salvation; therefore, I am saved.

(Proverbs 3:5,6; Isaiah 53:4,5; 1 Peter 2:24; Romans 10:8-13)

JEREMIAH 30:12-17

"For thus says the LORD: 'Your affliction is incurable, your wound is severe. There is no one to plead your cause, that you may be bound up; you have no healing medicines. All your lovers have forgotten you; they do not seek you; for I have wounded you with the wound of an enemy, with the chastisement of a cruel one, for the multitude of your iniquities, because your sins have increased. Why do you cry about your affliction? Your sorrow is incurable. Because of the multitude of your iniquities, because your sins have increased, I have done these things to you. Therefore all those who devour you shall be devoured; and all your adversaries, every one of them, shall go into captivity; those who plunder you shall become plunder, and all who prey upon you I will make a prey. For I will restore health to you and heal you of your wounds,' says the Lord, 'Because they called you an outcast saying: "This is Zion; No one seeks her."'"

~ PRAYER ~

Father, You sought me and found me, and I have responded to Your love. You have turned the attacks of Satan back on his own head.

Those who plundered me have become plunder. All of the demons who preyed upon me have now become my prey. For You have restored me to divine health and have healed all of my wounds. I am now an ambassador of Your goodness, Father, to declare Your praises to all of the earth.

──────── *DECLARATION OF FAITH* ────────

God has restored health and vitality to me and has healed all of my wounds. He has compassion on my dwelling and restores to me all of the fortunes that the devil robbed from my life. Good health, prosperity, and God's tender care are ever-present realities for me to enjoy.

(Exodus 15:26; Isaiah 53:5; 1 Peter 2:24; Joel 2:25; 2 Corinthians 8:9)

JEREMIAH 33:6-9

"'Behold, I will bring it health and healing; I will heal them and reveal to them the abundance of peace and truth. And I will cause the captives of Judah and the captives of Israel to return, and will rebuild those places as at the first. I will cleanse them from all their iniquity by which they have sinned against Me, and I will pardon all their iniquities by which they have sinned and by which they have transgressed against Me. Then it shall be to Me a name of joy, a praise, and an honor before all nations of the earth, who shall hear all the good that I do to them; they shall fear and tremble for all the goodness and all the prosperity that I provide for it.'"

~ *PRAYER* ~

Father, thank You for bringing me health and healing. You have healed me and revealed to me the abundance of peace and truth. I was once held captive to Satan's whims, but I have been set free! All of my sins and iniquities were placed upon Jesus and I now have the right to Your healing power. What a joy it is to be a son/daughter in Your household. I will testify of the good things You have done for me, Father. I present my life as an example of the goodness of my God!

———— DECLARATION OF FAITH ————

My Father has brought perfect health and healing to me and allows me to enjoy abundant peace and security. I am cleansed of all sin and forgiven of all of my rebellion against God. At this very moment, I stand in His presence as holy as Jesus himself. This puts a smile on God's face and frees Him to do what He has wanted to do all along: be a Father to me and bless me with my portion of His inheritance.

It gives my Father tremendous joy to bless me with all good things. Not only this, but He also receives praise, honor, and great renown among those who hear of what He has done for me. Their mouths gape in astonishment at the abundant prosperity and peace that He provides for His children.

(Hebrews 10:14-17; 2 Corinthians 5:17-21; 1 John 4:17; Romans 8:14-17; 14:17; Galatians 4:5,6; Deuteronomy 28:1-14; 1 Peter 2:24; Ephesians 2:14; James 5:14-16; Psalm 91)

CHAPTER TWELVE

EZEKIEL

EZEKIEL 34:1-4

The word of the LORD came to me, saying, "Son of man, prophesy against the shepherds of Israel, prophesy and say to them, 'Thus says the Lord GOD to the shepherds: "Woe to the shepherds of Israel who feed themselves! Should not the shepherds feed the flocks? You eat the fat and clothe yourselves with the wool; you slaughter the fatlings, but you do not feed the flock. The weak you have not strengthened, nor have you healed those who were sick, nor bound up the broken, nor brought back what was driven away, nor sought what was lost; but with force and cruelty you have ruled them.'"

~ PRAYER ~

Father, Your heart is so evident in the words of this passage. You truly care deeply for Your children. You care deeply for me. I know that in You there is strength for the day. You are quick with Your healing power. You bind up my wounds and comfort me in my troubles. You seek me out when I stray and hold me as Your very own. I gladly bow my knee before You, Father. You alone are worthy of my praise.

———— *DECLARATION OF FAITH* ————

I will not allow selfishness to rule my walk with God. Service dictates my every motive. I serve God, His children, and yes, even the world. God through me heals the sick, strengthens the weak, and gives comfort for the hurting. I am on an impassioned quest for those who have strayed from God's tender embrace and I am a grappler for the lost souls of the earth.

(Job 29:15-17,21-24; Isaiah 61:1-3; Daniel 12:3; Luke 15:4; 1 Peter 5:2,3)

EZEKIEL 34:11-16

"'For thus says the Lord GOD: "Indeed I Myself will search for My sheep and seek them out. As a shepherd seeks out his flock on the day he is among his scattered sheep, so will I seek out My sheep and deliver them from all the places where they were scattered on a cloudy and dark day. And I will bring them out from the peoples and gather them from the countries, and will bring them to their own land; I will feed them on the mountains of Israel, in the valleys and in all the inhabited places of the country. I will feed them in good pasture, and their fold shall be on the high mountains of Israel. There they shall lie down in a good fold and feed in rich pasture on the mountains of Israel. I will feed My flock, and I will make them lie down," says the Lord GOD. "I will seek what was lost and bring back what was driven away, bind up the broken and strengthen what was sick; but I will destroy the fat and the strong, and feed them in judgment.'"""

~ PRAYER ~

Father, thank You for seeking me out. I was like a sheep who had gone astray. I walked in my own way and in accordance with the dictates of my own heart. I had no desire for You. But You loved me so much that You sought me out and found me. You gathered me to Yourself and changed my heart. I gave You no reason to want me, yet You called me to be Your own. I am so grateful for Your love. Your kindness and mercy are my treasure. I am now Your son/daughter and heir. You feed me in rich, green pastures and I lie down in a good fold. You have healed my aching body and my broken heart. I live by Your strength and Your love ever sustains me. I will praise You forever.

──── DECLARATION OF FAITH ────

My Father's protective eye never leaves me. He looks after me as a good shepherd looks after his flock when he is with them.

The Lord is my Shepherd. He sets me in a fertile pasture and tends to my every need. He sees to it that I have nothing but the best from His great storehouse of provision. He heals my every sickness and comforts me in times of sadness. He grants me tremendous strength to overcome my weaknesses and He shepherds me with His justice.

(John 10:10-18; Matthew 8:17; 2 Corinthians 1:3,4; Colossians 1:29; Nehemiah 1:5,6; Job 36:7; Psalms 3:5,6; 11:4; 23)

EZEKIEL 47:8-12

Then he said to me: "This water flows toward the eastern region, goes down into the valley, and enters the sea. When it reaches the sea, its waters are healed. And it shall be that every living thing that moves, wherever the rivers go, will live. There will be a very great multitude of fish, because these waters go there; for they will be healed, and everything will live wherever the river goes. It shall be that fishermen will stand by it from En Gedi to En Eglaim; they will be places for spreading their nets. Their fish will be of the same kinds as the fish of the Great Sea, exceedingly many. But its swamps and marshes will not be healed; they will be given over to salt. Along the bank of the river, on this side and that, will grow all kinds of trees used for food; their leaves will not wither, and their fruit will not fail. They will bear fruit every month, because their water flows from the sanctuary. Their fruit will be for food, and their leaves for medicine."

~ PRAYER ~

Father, I know that this verse is indicative of the rivers of living water that represent Your Holy Spirit. Wherever these waters go there is healing and everything will live where the river flows. Therefore, I shall live, Father. Out of my belly flows rivers of living water! You give life to this mortal body by the Holy Spirit who dwells within me.

Father, You have thoroughly established Yourself as my great Healer. You love me and have no desire to see me sick, fearful, or depressed. Therefore, I will walk in Your healing, in Jesus' name.

——— DECLARATION OF FAITH ———

I live in the flow of the Holy Spirit. His life-giving waters are refreshment for my soul. He brings me healing wherever He is, and by the grace of God He lives within me. He even provides medicines in the vegetation around me to ensure that my health is sustained. He hates sickness and disease and does all that He can to provide for my healing.

(1 Timothy 5:23; Romans 8:11; John 7:37-39; Job 29:2-6; Psalm 1:3; Zechariah 14:8; Isaiah 12:3)

CHAPTER THIRTEEN

HOSEA

HOSEA 6:1,2

Come, and let us return to the LORD; for He has torn, but He will heal us; He has stricken, but He will bind us up. After two days He will revive us; on the third day He will raise us up, that we may live in His sight.

~ PRAYER ~

Father, it is a joy to be living in the time of Your grace. I never have to worry about Your judgment. I now enjoy healing and prosperity. You have revived me that I may live in Your sight—all praise to Your holy name.

——— DECLARATION OF FAITH ———

I have become God's own son/daughter and He has healed all of my infirmities. In Him, I am made whole in every way.

He has restored me in righteousness so that I may enter His presence without any sense of guilt or inadequacy.

I will continually acknowledge His presence in my life. As surely as the sun rises He is with me, and He rains His blessings upon me freely.

(Galatians 3:13; 4:5,6; Isaiah 53:5; 2 Corinthians 5:21; Hebrews 4:16)

HOSEA 11:3,4

"I taught Ephraim to walk, taking them by their arms; but they did not know that I healed them. I drew them with gentle cords, with bands of love, and I was to them as those who take the yoke from their neck. I stooped and fed them."

~ *PRAYER* ~

Lord, I thank You for being a gentle, loving Father to me. You take me in Your arms and draw me with gentle cords and bands of love. You took the yoke off my neck and stooped down to feed me. You have declared that every wound that Jesus suffered was for me and that by those wounds I am made whole. You are awesome, Father, and so very worthy of my praise.

—— DECLARATION OF FAITH ——

The Lord takes me into His gentle arms and heals me of every sickness. He leads me with a familiar kindness and with ties of love. He gives me the ability to stand rock solid so that I can do His will in every situation. He lifts the heavy burden from my shoulders and nourishes me until my vitality returns and I am once again able to enjoy the gift of His salvation.

(Deuteronomy 33:12; James 5:14,15; Romans 5:1,2; John 16:13; Matthew 11:28,29; Isaiah 40:28-31)

HOSEA 14:4-7

"I will heal their backsliding, I will love them freely, for My anger has turned away from him. I will be like the dew to Israel; he shall grow like the lily, and lengthen his roots like Lebanon. His branches shall spread; his beauty shall be like an olive tree, and his fragrance like Lebanon. Those who dwell under his shadow shall return; they shall be revived like grain, and grow like a vine. Their scent shall be like the wine of Lebanon."

~ PRAYER ~

Father, I thank You for Your mercy and grace. Your anger is turned away from me. It was all placed on Jesus two thousand years ago. Now You are free to love me without restraint. You are free to prosper me and bring me health. I am like revived grain dwelling under Your shadow and I grow like a vine.

—— DECLARATION OF FAITH ——

My Father has given me direction and freedom. He has healed all of my waywardness and has set His unconditional, everlasting love upon me for all of eternity. His anger will never be turned my way again. His renewing grace is like morning dew watering my ground and I blossom like a lily in the spring (fast-growing and full of fragrance and beauty), but with roots like the cedars of Lebanon (so deep that I can never be plucked up).

(Proverbs 3:5,6; Galatians 5:1; Titus 3:5; Jeremiah 14:7; Ephesians 1:6; John 10:27-30)

CHAPTER FOURTEEN

JOEL

JOEL 3:9,10

Proclaim this among the nations: "Prepare for war! Wake up the mighty men, let all the men of war draw near, let them come up. Beat your plowshares into swords and your pruning hooks into spears; let the weak say, 'I am strong.'"

~ PRAYER ~

Father, prepare me for battle. Teach my hands to war and my fingers to fight. Make me aware of the enemy's schemes and his attempts to take control of my tongue. I declare in accordance with Your Word that I am strong in You. In Jesus' name, I will prevail in this fight and continue to advance Your kingdom without hindrance.

—— DECLARATION OF FAITH ——

Though my victory has been sealed and the struggle for freedom is over for me, there is still a war going on and I intend to fight it. I

prepare myself daily for the battle, rousing myself to a condition of per-
petual vigilance.

When the enemy raises his ugly head, I attack him without mercy.

All of my sowing and reaping suddenly becomes a deadly weapon.

I will not allow the weaknesses, failures, or foolishness of my past
to hinder me. I stand and declare myself to be what God says I am. I
am strong in the Lord and in the power of His might and well able to
defeat the enemy on any ground!

(1 Corinthians 15:57; Ephesians 6:10-18; 2 Timothy 1:6,7; Philippians 3:12-14;
Psalm 144:1)

CHAPTER FIFTEEN

MALACHI

MALACHI 4:2

But to you who fear My name the Sun of Righteousness shall arise with healing in His wings; and you shall go out and grow fat like stall-fed calves.

~ PRAYER ~

Father, I trust in the power of Jesus' name. My Savior is risen with healing in His wings. His name is above all sickness and disease. Through Him I go out and flourish like a stall-fed calf. I am under the care of the Almighty and nothing shall by any means harm me.

DECLARATION OF FAITH

Jesus, my Lord, my Sun of Righteousness, has risen with healing in His wings.

I stand secure in the power of His name.

I have been revived, healed, and reborn.

I go out leaping like a calf released from the stall.

I am now a master of the forces of darkness. They are nothing more than ashes beneath my feet.

(2 Corinthians 4:6; 5:21; Matthew 4:16; Ephesians 5:14; John 3:3; Titus 3:5; Luke 10:17-19; Psalm 91:13)

CHAPTER SIXTEEN

MATTHEW

✠

MATTHEW 4:23,24

Jesus went about all Galilee, teaching in their synagogues, preaching the gospel of the kingdom, and healing all kinds of sickness and all kinds of disease among the people. Then His fame went throughout all Syria; and they brought to Him all sick people who were afflicted with various diseases and torments, and those who were demon-possessed, epileptics, and paralytics; and He healed them.

~ PRAYER ~

Father, I have Your Word that no matter what comes against me, in Jesus' name I can overcome it. Demons cannot possess me, epilepsy cannot control me, and paralysis cannot stop me. I am in Jesus, and by His stripes I am healed.

——— DECLARATION OF FAITH ———

Jesus has healed all of my sicknesses and diseases. No matter what the affliction is that comes against me, He has provided my healing through the power of His name. I can no longer be tormented. I am free!

(Isaiah 53:3-5; 61:1-3; Acts 3:1-10)

MATTHEW 8:1-4

When He had come down from the mountain, great multitudes followed Him. And behold, a leper came and worshiped Him, saying, "Lord, if You are willing, You can make me clean." Then Jesus put out His hand and touched him, saying, "I am willing; be cleansed." Immediately his leprosy was cleansed. And Jesus said to him, "See that you tell no one; but go your way, show yourself to the priest, and offer the gift that Moses commanded, as a testimony to them."

~ *PRAYER* ~

Father, this verse forever settles the question of whether or not You are willing to heal me. Jesus' only purpose was to do Your will. Therefore, I know that You want me well, and I will not allow the devil or anyone else to try to convince me otherwise.

──── *DECLARATION OF FAITH* ────

My Father is more than willing to bring His healing power into my body so that I can walk in perfect wholeness in this life.

(Isaiah 53:4,5; 1 Peter 2:24; James 5:14-16; Exodus 15:26; Psalm 103:1-5; John 4:34)

MATTHEW 8:5-13

Now when Jesus had entered Capernaum, a centurion came to Him, pleading with Him, saying, "Lord, my servant is lying at home paralyzed, dreadfully tormented." And Jesus said to him, "I will come and heal him." The centurion answered and said, "Lord, I am not worthy that You should come under my roof. But only speak a word, and my servant will be healed. For I also am a man under authority, having soldiers under me. And I say to this one, 'Go,' and he goes; and to another, 'Come,' and he comes; and to my servant, 'Do this,' and he does it." When Jesus heard it, He marveled, and said to those who followed, "Assuredly, I say to you, I have not found such great faith, not even in Israel! And I say to you that many will come from east and west, and sit down with Abraham, Isaac, and Jacob in the kingdom of heaven. But the sons of the kingdom will be cast out into outer darkness. There will be weeping and gnashing of teeth." Then Jesus said to the centurion, "Go your way; and as you have believed, so let it be done for you." And his servant was healed that same hour.

~ PRAYER ~

Father, Your love and willingness to heal is so evident in Your Word. You are quick to respond to my faith. Therefore, I speak to my body now and command it to be healed:

Body, I do not permit you to be sick any longer. You will obey the Word and submit yourself to health and prosperity, in Jesus' name!

Father, I thank You that Your healing power is flowing through me. Your Word is at work within me, and it will accomplish the task You have sent it forth to do.

———— *DECLARATION OF FAITH* ————

When I speak the Word of God, His healing power occupies my words and is carried into the body of the one who has faith.

Words are my servants and the carriers of my faith to a hurting world.

My faith works for me according to what I believe. What I believe I have received, that is what I shall have.

(Mark 9:23; 11:22-25; 2 Corinthians 4:13; Romans 10:8-10; Hebrews 11:1; Psalm 107:20; Proverbs 18:20,21; Isaiah 55:11)

MATTHEW 8:14,15

Now when Jesus had come into Peter's house, He saw his wife's mother lying sick with a fever. So He touched her hand, and the fever left her. And she arose and served them.

~ PRAYER ~

Father, I thank You for the power to overcome fever.

—— DECLARATION OF FAITH ——

Fever is no match for the power of Jesus' name. Therefore, my body temperature shall remain normal.

(Mark 1:30,31; Luke 4:38,39; John 4:52; Acts 28:8)

MATTHEW 8:16,17

When evening had come, they brought to Him many who were demon-possessed. And He cast out the spirits with a word, and healed all who were sick, that it might be fulfilled which was spoken by Isaiah the prophet, saying: "He Himself took our infirmities and bore our sicknesses."

~ PRAYER ~

Father, I know that You stand with me at all times and through every circumstance. You are my personal trainer in spiritual warfare and You back my every move. Jesus bore my sicknesses and carried my pains. Any infirmity in my body is there contrary to Your will. Therefore, I take my authority over Satan and his demons:

Satan, I command you and every evil spirit to leave my body. I will not tolerate your foul sicknesses any longer. Leave me now, in Jesus' name!

—— DECLARATION OF FAITH ——

I use my words to drive out demons and restore health to myself and those in my circle of influence.

Jesus shouldered all of my weaknesses and carried away all of my diseases.

(Isaiah 53:4,5; 1 Peter 2:24; Exodus 15:26; John 14:12; Psalm 107:20; Mark 16:17-20; Proverbs 18:20,21)

MATTHEW 9:1-8

So He got into a boat, crossed over, and came to His own city. Then behold, they brought to Him a paralytic lying on a bed. When Jesus saw their faith, he said to the paralytic, "Son, be of good cheer; your sins are forgiven you." And at once some of the scribes said within themselves, "This Man blasphemes!" But Jesus, knowing their thoughts, said, "Why do you think evil in your hearts? For which is easier, to say, 'Your sins are forgiven you,' or to say, 'Arise and walk'? But that you may know that the Son of Man has power on earth to forgive sins"—then He said to the paralytic, "Arise, take up your bed, and go to your house." And he arose and departed to his house. Now when the multitudes saw it, they marveled and glorified God, who had given such power to men.

~ PRAYER ~

Father, I thank You that in Jesus I have forgiveness of my sins. You do not look at my own worthiness as a reason to heal me. I receive Your healing by grace through faith. Look to me, Father. See that I have faith to be healed. Magnify Your anointing in my body. Give me a testimony of Your great love that others may marvel and give You glory.

Paralysis is no match for the healing power of my God. As long as I have faith, I have the keys that unlock God's power to work in my life. Therefore, in spite of my circumstances, I declare that I am healed!

(Acts 28:8; James 5:13-16; Isaiah 33:24)

MATTHEW 9:18-25

While He spoke these things to them, behold, a ruler came and worshiped Him, saying, "My daughter has just died, but come and lay Your hand on her and she will live." So Jesus arose and followed him, and so did His disciples. And suddenly, a woman who had a flow of blood for twelve years came from behind and touched the hem of His garment. For she said to herself, "If only I may touch His garment, I shall be made well." But Jesus turned around, and when He saw her He said, "Be of good cheer, daughter; your faith has made you well." And the woman was made well from that hour. When Jesus came into the ruler's house, and saw the flute players and the noisy crowd wailing, He said to them, "Make room, for the girl is not dead, but sleeping." And they ridiculed Him. But when the crowd was put outside, He went in and took her by the hand, and the girl arose.

~ PRAYER ~

Father, I am determined to be persistent with my faith. I will not turn from Your Word. You have said that I am healed. Therefore, I am healed. I have reason to rejoice even in the midst of my suffering, for

I have Your unfailing Word that my faith has made me well. I praise You, in spite of my circumstances, Father. I lift You up, exalt and magnify Your holy name. Others can mock and ridicule me all they want; they will soon be silenced when they see me healed.

———— *DECLARATION OF FAITH* ————

I stand on the Word as my final authority. No matter what I am facing, my faith can make me well.

(Philippians 4:4-13; James 5:14-16; Luke 7:50; 8:48)

MATTHEW 9:27–30

When Jesus departed from there, two blind men followed Him, crying out and saying, "Son of David, have mercy on us!" And when He had come into the house, the blind men came to Him. And Jesus said to them, "Do you believe that I am able to do this?" They said to Him, "Yes, Lord." Then He touched their eyes, saying, "According to your faith let it be to you." And their eyes were opened.

~ *PRAYER* ~

Father, Your system has limitless possibilities. You can easily do anything You want to do. All You ask is that I have faith that You can and will do it. I believe in You, Lord. I trust in Your power and unfailing love. I now choose to walk in my healing, in Jesus' name.

—— *DECLARATION OF FAITH* ——

I firmly believe in the power and ability of God that is within me.
According to my faith (my believing and speaking the answer), all of
my needs and godly desires become a reality in my life.

(Colossians 1:29; Ephesians 1:17-23; 2 Corinthians 4:13; Philippians 4:19;
Hebrews 11:1)

MATTHEW 9:35,36

Then Jesus went about all the cities and villages, teaching in their synagogues, preaching the gospel of the kingdom, and healing every sickness and every disease among the people. But when He saw the
multitudes, He was moved with compassion for them, because they
were weary and scattered, like sheep having no shepherd.

~ *PRAYER* ~

Father, I clearly see how much You love me and want me well. You are
a good Father to me. You have healed me of every sickness and every
disease. I cling to You with every fiber of my strength. I am no longer
as a sheep without a shepherd. I am encompassed and guarded by my
own Father: the very Lord of the universe!

—— *DECLARATION OF FAITH* ——

I am an ambassador of Christ—the very avenue that God has
chosen to bring His power into the earth. I am anointed with His own

ability to preach the good news of His kingdom and to heal all kinds of diseases and every kind of weakness and infirmity.

(John 14:12; 2 Corinthians 5:17-20; Luke 10:19; Ephesians 1:17-23; 1 John 2:20; Matthew 10:1)

MATTHEW 10:1

And when He had called His twelve disciples to Him, He gave them power over unclean spirits, to cast them out, and to heal all kinds of sickness and all kinds of disease.

~ *PRAYER* ~

Father, I thank You for giving me power and authority over and above all of the power and authority of the enemy. I thank You that demons of sickness and disease are subject to me in Christ. I exercise that anointing now:

Satan, I command you and all of your demons to take your filthy sicknesses away from my presence. I bind you, devil! I cast you out according to the Word of my Father. I bind your sicknesses and loose healing into my body, in Jesus' name!

———— DECLARATION OF FAITH ————

*I have been given power and authority over **all** evil spirits. They must obey my commands in the name of Jesus. I drive out all demons* *from my presence, and heal all kinds of diseases and every kind of weakness and infirmity.*

(John 14:12; 1 John 4:4; Luke 10:18:19; Ephesians 1:17-23; Mark 16:17-20)

MATTHEW 10:7,8

"As you go, preach, saying, 'The kingdom of heaven is at hand.' Heal the sick, cleanse the lepers, raise the dead, cast out demons. Freely you have received, freely give."

~ PRAYER ~

Father, You have freely given me all things that pertain unto life and godliness. Your kingdom is within me and there is no sickness in it. Since there is no sickness in Your kingdom, there is no sickness in me. I bind it and cast it out of my life, in Jesus' name.

——— DECLARATION OF FAITH ———

I proclaim the present reality of the kingdom of heaven wherever I go. In Jesus' name I heal the sick, raise the dead, cast out demons, and cleanse the lepers. Freely I have received this, and freely I give it.

(John 14:12; Isaiah 61:1-3; Matthew 3:2; Acts 8:18; Mark 16:15-20)

MATTHEW 11:4-6

Jesus answered and said to them, "Go and tell John the things which you hear and see: The blind see and the lame walk; the lepers are cleansed and the deaf hear; the dead are raised up and the poor have the gospel preached to them. And blessed is he who is not offended because of Me."

~ PRAYER ~

Father, I am not offended because of Jesus. He is the very Lord of my healing. All that I am and all that I need are found in Him. I am in Him, Father. Since He is not sick, I am not sick. I know the gospel. It is the good news of freedom and restoration. It is news of prosperity, peace, and divine health. Your own Word has declared it, Father, and I choose to walk in it.

——— DECLARATION OF FAITH ———

I am not offended at the gospel of my Lord Jesus. He is the healer of the lame, the leper, the sick, and the deaf. He raises the dead and gives life to all who call upon Him. I am not ashamed to call Him my brother. He is my Lord and I am delighted to be called by His name.

(Matthew 10:32,33; Romans 1:16; Acts 17:27,28; Hebrews 2:11)

MATTHEW 12:14-21

Then the Pharisees went out and plotted against Him, how they might destroy Him. But when Jesus knew it, He withdrew from there. And great multitudes followed Him, and He healed them all. Yet He warned them not to make Him known, that it might be fulfilled which was spoken by Isaiah the prophet, saying: "Behold! My Servant whom I have chosen, My Beloved in whom My soul is well pleased! I will put My Spirit upon Him, and He will declare justice to the Gentiles. He will not quarrel nor cry out, nor will anyone hear His voice in the streets. A bruised reed He will not break, and smoking flax He will not quench, till He sends forth justice to victory; and in His name Gentiles will trust."

~ PRAYER ~

Father, I thank You for the wonder and the privilege of having the right to use Jesus' name. No matter what I am facing, I know that in the name of Jesus I have the victory.

Father, I also thank You that I am in Him. In Jesus I live and move and have my being. He has given me the Spirit, with all of His ability, and He is dwelling within me at this very moment. This charges my faith, Father. This is the very Word of health and prosperity. Christ is in me and by His anointing I am saved, delivered, and healed!

—— DECLARATION OF FAITH ——

I have the right to use the name of Jesus to overcome any sickness, disease, malady, or disaster in my life. I don't have to rely upon my own name, nor do I have to trust in my own ability to earn a healing. All of my trust is in the name of Jesus. He is my righteousness, my wisdom, my sanctification, and my redemption. With Him as the surety of my healing, I can rest assured that I am truly healed.

(Psalms 103:1-5; 107:20; John 14:13-18; Philippians 2:9-11; Colossians 3:17)

MATTHEW 12:22

Then one was brought to Him who was demon-possessed, blind and mute; and He healed him, so that the blind and mute man both spoke and saw.

~ PRAYER ~

Father, I know that there is not a single circumstance that is beyond Your power to overcome. Blindness is no match for You. Demons are no match for You. All manner of sicknesses and diseases are no match for You. Therefore, anything that exalts itself against the knowledge of Your will I declare to be null and void in my life.

—— DECLARATION OF FAITH ——

In Jesus, the spirits of blindness and muteness have no power over me. In Him, I can see and talk as well as any other.

(1 Peter 2:24; James 5:14-16; Luke 10:18,19; 11:14,15; Psalm 103:1-5)

MATTHEW 13:10-23

And the disciples came and said to Him, "Why do You speak to them in parables?" He answered and said to them, "Because it has been given to you to know the mysteries of the kingdom of heaven, but to them it has not been given. For whoever has, to him more will be given, and he will have abundance; but whoever does not have, even what he has will be taken away from him. Therefore I speak to them in parables, because seeing they do not see, and hearing they do not hear, nor do they understand. And in them the prophecy of Isaiah is fulfilled, which says: 'Hearing you will hear and shall not understand, and seeing you will see and not perceive; for the hearts of this people have grown dull. Their ears are hard of hearing, and their eyes they have closed, lest they should see with their eyes and hear with their ears, lest they should understand with their hearts and turn, so that I should heal them.' But blessed are your eyes for they see, and your ears for they hear; for assuredly, I say to you that many prophets and righteous men desired to see what you see, and did not see it, and to hear what you hear, and did not hear it. Therefore hear the parable of the sower: When anyone hears the word of the kingdom, and does not understand it, then the wicked one comes and snatches away what was sown in his heart. This is he who received seed by the wayside. But he who received the seed on stony places, this is he who hears the word and immediately receives it with joy; yet he has no root in himself, but endures only for a while. For when tribulation or persecution arises because of the word, immediately he stumbles. Now he who received seed among the thorns is he who hears the word, and the cares of this world and the deceitfulness of riches choke the word, and he becomes unfruitful. But he who received seed on the good ground is he who hears the word and understands it, who indeed bears fruit and produces: some a hundredfold, some sixty, some thirty."

~ PRAYER ~

Father, I thank You that You have blessed my eyes to see and my ears to hear. I have revelation knowledge of Your Word and know of a certainty that Your healing power is mine to receive by faith. Father, I set my face like a flint to be steadfast and committed to Your Word. I will not allow Satan to deceive me and snatch the Word from me. No matter what kind of tribulation arises, I will not turn from it. I root the Word deep in my spirit, Father. I am not going to allow myself to endure for only a short while. I endure for all of eternity! I will not allow myself to ever turn from Your Word! Help me to maintain my focus, Father. Speak to me in the night seasons. Bring to my remembrance everything You have taught me. Father, I declare right now that I am good ground! I hear the Word, understand it, and bear an abundance of fruit, to the praise of Your name!

——— DECLARATION OF FAITH ———

God has given me the ability to know secrets and mysteries of the kingdom of heaven. I have been given a vast supply of wisdom and knowledge, and God is continually pouring more and more into my life so that I can be furnished richly and live in the fullness of His laws of abundance.

The eyes of my understanding have been enlightened. God's Word has been opened up to me. I can now see with eyes of discernment and hear with ears of comprehension. I understand and recognize the things of the Spirit.

I am receptive of God's healing power.

I am blessed, happy, fortunate, and to be envied, because I have the God-given ability to see and hear things as they truly are.

I hear and understand the specific details that God has revealed in His Word so that I may do what it leads me to do. I continually yield an abundant harvest in my life—even as much as one hundred times what I have sown.

(Matthew 13:11; 25:29; James 1:22-25; Genesis 26:12; 2 Corinthians 9:5-11; Malachi 3:10; Luke 8:10; 1 Corinthians 2:6-16; Daniel 1:4,17,20; 2:22,23; John 10:10; Ephesians 1:17-23; Psalm 107:20; 1 John 2:20; 5:20)

Matthew 13:31,32

Another parable [Jesus] put forth to them, saying: "The kingdom of heaven is like a mustard seed, which a man took and sowed in his field, which indeed is the least of all the seeds; but when it is grown it is greater than the herbs and becomes a tree, so that the birds of the air come and nest in its branches."

~ *PRAYER* ~

Thank You, Father, for revelation knowledge of Your kingdom. By this verse, I see a principle of faith. By sowing Your Word persistently and patiently, I can uproot any problem that I face.

──────── *DECLARATION OF FAITH* ────────

I operate the principles of the kingdom in the spirit of faith that have been given to me. I understand that when I sow kingdom principles,

they are like grains of mustard seed. Though they are small in the midst
of all other seeds that have been sown into my life, through faith and
patience I can water them until their roots have choked out all that
does not bring glory to God. In this manner, I receive such an abun-
dance of blessings that I have all that I need and plenty left over so that
my life becomes a refuge to everyone in my circle of influence.

(Galatians 6:9; 2 Corinthians 4:13; 9:5-11; Hebrews 6:12; Luke 13:18,19;
Genesis 12:3)

MATTHEW 14:14

When Jesus went out He saw a great multitude; and He was moved
with compassion for them, and healed their sick.

~ *PRAYER* ~

Father God, I am humbled by Your great love for me. You are a
loving Father and have no desire to see me sick. I trust in Your love,
Father. I know that You want me well. Therefore, by Your Word, I
receive my healing.

——— *DECLARATION OF FAITH* ———

My Lord has tremendous compassion for me and is more than
willing to provide my healing when I need it.

(Psalms 103:1-5,13; 107:20; James 5:14-16; Exodus 15:26; 23:25)

MATTHEW 14:35,36

When the men of that place recognized [Jesus], they sent out into all that surrounding region, brought to Him all who were sick, and begged Him that they might only touch the hem of His garment. And as many as touched it were made perfectly well.

~ PRAYER ~

Father, You are so good to me. You meet me where I am and work with me at a level that I can understand. You work wherever there is faith. If I need to focus on the hem of a garment, You will work with that. If I can hold fast to the spoken Word, You will work with that as well. All that You require is that I have faith. I believe, Father, and I will act on that belief, in Jesus' name.

——— DECLARATION OF FAITH ———

God is so devoted to my healing that He will use whatever means of faith that I can cling to in order to make me well.

(Acts 15:12-16; 19:11,12; James 5:13-16; Psalm 107:20; Matthew 8:8)

MATTHEW 15:22-28

And behold, a woman of Canaan came from that region and cried out to Him, saying, "Have mercy on me, O Lord, Son of David! My daughter is severely demon-possessed." But He answered her not a word. And His disciples came and urged Him, saying, "Send her away, for she cries out after us." But He answered and said, "I was not sent except to the lost sheep of the house of Israel." Then she came and worshiped Him, saying, "Lord, help me!" But He answered and said, "It is not good to take the children's bread and throw it to the little dogs." And she said, "Yes, Lord, yet even the little dogs eat the crumbs which fall from their masters' table." Then Jesus answered and said to her, "O woman, great is your faith! Let it be to you as you desire." And her daughter was healed from that very hour.

~ *PRAYER* ~

Father, You call healing "the children's bread." That means it absolutely belongs to Your kids. And yet, You will not even withhold it from an outsider if they will but exercise faith. I see this clearly, Father. You want me well, and as a good Father, You have provided the sustenance of healing power to nourish me in this life. You are quick to respond to my faith. Therefore, I now receive my healing from the table of Your blessings.

—— *DECLARATION OF FAITH* ——

I have been given a tremendous measure of faith and I am persistent, even tenacious, with it, until I receive what it is that I am asking for.

(Romans 12:3; Matthew 7:7-11; 18:7,8; Hebrews 10:35-11:1,6; Psalm 23:5)

MATTHEW 15:30-31

Then great multitudes came to Him, having with them the lame, blind, mute, maimed, and many others; and they laid them down at

Jesus' feet, and He healed them. So the multitude marveled when they saw the mute speaking, the maimed made whole, the lame walking, and the blind seeing; and they glorified the God of Israel.

~ PRAYER ~

Father, Your Word is strong. There is no area of malady or infirmity that it does not cover. Nothing is exempt from Your healing power. Father, I just read it and I choose to believe it. I'm not going to reason against Your Word. It's right there in front of my eyes. You make the mute speak, the maimed are made whole, the lame walk, the blind see, and all others are included as well. I'm in this, Father. I step up right now and name my healing. I am Your covenant child. Healing belongs to me and that's all there is to it.

——— DECLARATION OF FAITH ———

I serve the God of all healing. Nothing is exempt from His power and ability, nor is there any type of malady that is outside of His will to heal. I choose to believe this and I claim my healing, in Jesus name!

(Ephesians 1:19-23; Isaiah 55:11; Deuteronomy 28:15-68)

MATTHEW 16:19

"I will give you the keys of the kingdom of heaven, and whatever you bind on earth will be bound in heaven, and whatever you loose on earth will be loosed in heaven."

~ *PRAYER* ~

Father, I thank You for the keys that unlock Your blessings in my life. What is bound in heaven I can bind on earth, and what is loosed in heaven I can loose on earth. Lord, I'm standing with You right now and I say that Your will shall be done on earth as it is in heaven! So let me take inventory, Father. There is no sickness, disease, poverty, or calamities in heaven, so I now bind them in my life! Healing is an ever-present fact in heaven, so I now loose it into my body, in Jesus' name.

———— *DECLARATION OF FAITH* ————

I have the keys of the kingdom of heaven. I can bind on earth what is bound in heaven and I can loose on earth what is loosed in heaven. I set myself in harmony and agreement with heaven and I live a healthy, prosperous, long life as the days of heaven are upon the earth.

(Matthew 4:17; 6:10; 18:18; Deuteronomy 11:21; 30:19)

MATTHEW 20:30-34

And behold, two blind men sitting by the road, when they heard that Jesus was passing by, cried out, saying, "Have mercy on us, O Lord, Son of David!" Then the multitude warned them that they should be quiet; but they cried out all the more, saying, "Have mercy on us, O Lord, Son of David!" So Jesus stood still and called them, and said, "What do you want Me to do for you?" They said to Him, "Lord, that our eyes may be opened." So Jesus had compassion and touched their eyes. And immediately their eyes received sight, and they followed Him.

~ *PRAYER* ~

Father, I am not concerned with what others think of my faith. I would rather please You than fickle men. When others tell me to stop what I am doing, I will cry out to You all the more! You are the source of all salvation. Any healing that I receive finds its origin in You.

Father, I also thank You for Your grace and mercy towards me. You don't see me as a sin-ridden worm, but as a precious treasure. You love me with a depth of compassion that the world cannot fathom. I trust in that compassion, Father. All I have to do is ask in faith and You give me the desires of my heart.

——— *DECLARATION OF FAITH* ———

I know the One in whom I believe. I focus my attention on Him and not the crowd.

When I am reproved for my faith and told to be still, I cry out all the more, praying and shouting to the only One who can set me free.

My Lord is alert to my every cry. He notices me. He wants me to tell Him specifically what I desire from Him so my joy will be complete when He gives it to me. When I give Him my specific request, in harmony with His Word, He calls it done.

(2 Timothy 1:12; John 14:13,14; 15:7; 16:23,24; Matthew 19:13,14)

MATTHEW 21:14

Then the blind and the lame came to Him in the temple, and He healed them.

~ PRAYER ~

Father, You have not placed blindness or paralysis outside of Your will to heal. I know that all manner of healing is mine if I will but exercise the anointing in faith.

—— DECLARATION OF FAITH ——

Jesus has healed my vision and cured any damage to my body that could make me lame.

(Exodus 15:26; 23:25; Isaiah 53:4,5; Acts 5:16; 8:7; Matthew 4:23)

MATTHEW 21:21,22

So Jesus answered and said to them, "Assuredly, I say to you, if you have faith and do not doubt, you will not only do what was done to the fig tree, but also if you say to this mountain, 'Be removed and be cast into the sea,' it will be done. And whatever things you ask in prayer, believing, you will receive."

~ PRAYER ~

Father, thank You for believing in me. Your Word says that if I have faith and do not doubt, I will have the things that I say. Therefore, in spite of what my natural eye can see, I believe I receive my healing.

Your healing power is in my body at this very moment driving out all sickness, disease, and malady, in Jesus' name.

DECLARATION OF FAITH

I engage my faith by believing the Word and speaking it to the problem. My faith is pure and focused with a deep-seated belief free of all doubt. I know that when I believe in God's power within me I can speak to any problem and it must obey my command. Whatever I ask for in faith, if I believe I have received it, regardless of the circumstances, I shall have it.

(2 Corinthians 4:13; Mark 11:22-25; Hebrews 10:35-11:1; James 1:6-8)

CHAPTER SEVENTEEN

MARK

MARK 1:30,31

Simon's wife's mother lay sick with a fever, and they told [Jesus] about her at once. So He came and took her by the hand and lifted her up, and immediately the fever left her. And she served them.

~ PRAYER ~

Father, I thank You that fever is no match for Your anointing. By Your power, I am healed of fever.

——— DECLARATION OF FAITH ———

Fever must leave my body in Jesus' name. My body works perfectly, in the way that God intended when He made me. I will not allow the sickness of fever to taint the great work that He has done.

(Matthew 8:14,15; Luke 4:38,39; John 4:52,53; Acts 28:8)

MARK 1:32-34

At evening, when the sun had set, they brought to [Jesus] all who were sick and those who were demon-possessed. And the whole city was gathered together at the door. Then He healed many who were sick with various diseases, and cast out many demons; and He did not allow the demons to speak, because they knew Him.

~ PRAYER ~

Father, I thank You that I am in Christ Jesus and carry His very same authority. You have given me power over all of the power of the enemy and nothing shall by any means harm me. I stand before You now and exercise that power:

Satan, I command you and every demon to leave me now, in Jesus' name. You take your foul sicknesses and ailments away from me and my household. We are the healed of the Lord and we do not permit you to enter our presence.

——— DECLARATION OF FAITH ———

In Jesus, I am both healed and have the ability, through the anointing, to heal all sickness and disease.

I have the authority, in Jesus' name, to drive out all demons from my presence.

(1 Peter 2:24; Mark 16:17-20; Luke 10:18,19; Psalm 91:13)

MARK 1:40-42

Now a leper came to Him, imploring Him, kneeling down to Him and saying to Him, "If You are willing, You can make me clean." Then Jesus, moved with compassion, stretched out His hand and touched him, and said to him, "I am willing; be cleansed." As soon as He had spoken, immediately the leprosy left him, and he was cleansed.

~ PRAYER ~

Father, Your love for me is overwhelming. Knowing how much You care for me, regardless of what I have done, makes me tremble in amazement. You look to me as the apple of Your eye. You are quick to respond to my prayers and You pour out Your healing power on me without restraint. I don't have to worry about whether or not You are willing to heal me. Your love, as revealed in Your Word, is all the proof I need.

—— DECLARATION OF FAITH ——

Jesus is willing to heal all who are oppressed of the devil, and His healing power is available for me to receive by faith.

(Isaiah 61:1-3; Luke 10:18,19; James 5:14-16; Psalm 103:1-5; Luke 7:13; Romans 8:31-39)

MARK 2:3-12

Then they came to Him, bringing a paralytic who was carried by four men. And when they could not come near Him because of the crowd, they uncovered the roof where He was. So when they had broken through, they let down the bed on which the paralytic was lying. When Jesus saw their faith, He said to the paralytic, "Son, your sins are forgiven you." And some of the scribes were sitting there and reasoning in their hearts, "Why does this Man speak blasphemies like this? Who can forgive sins but God alone?" But immediately, when Jesus perceived in His spirit that they reasoned thus within themselves, He said to them, "Why do you reason about these things in your hearts? Which is easier, to say to the paralytic, 'Your sins are forgiven you,' or to say, 'Arise, take up your bed and walk'? But that you may know that the Son of Man has power on earth to forgive sins"—He said to the paralytic, "I say to you, arise, take up your bed, and go to your house." Immediately he arose, took up the bed, and went out in the presence of them all, so that all were amazed and glorified God, saying, "We never saw anything like this!"

~ PRAYER ~

Father, I thank You that all of my sins, from first to last, are forgiven. The barrier has been broken and the yoke of bondage has been shattered from off my neck. I now receive Your healing power freely and live my days in divine health and happiness, in Jesus' name.

——— DECLARATION OF FAITH ———

All of my sins—past, present, or future—are forgiven. By one sacrifice Jesus paid the price for them all. Now there is nothing that can prevent me from receiving, or make me unworthy of, God's healing power.

(Hebrews 10:14; Ephesians 1:7-12; Colossians 2:13-15; Romans 6:8-11; Galatians 2:20-3:6; 1 John 2:1,2)

MARK 3:1–5 (ALSO IN LUKE 6:6–11)

[Jesus] entered the synagogue again, and a man was there who had a withered hand. So they watched Him closely, whether He would heal him on the Sabbath, so that they might accuse Him. And He said to the man who had the withered hand, "Step forward." Then He said to them, "Is it lawful on the Sabbath to do good or to do evil, to save life or to kill?" But they kept silent. And when He had looked around at them with anger, being grieved by the hardness of their hearts, He said to the man, "Stretch out your hand." And he stretched it out, and his hand was restored as whole as the other.

~ PRAYER ~

Father, I thank You that You heal me regardless of what religious leaders think about it. No matter how many excuses they make for not allowing Your healing power to flow in their midst, I can still stand on Your Word and receive my healing, in Jesus' name.

—— DECLARATION OF FAITH ——

Religious leaders cannot stop me from being healed. I know that healing is good, and sickness and maladies are evil. I will not harden my heart against the heart of my God. In Jesus' name, I am made whole.

(Isaiah 53:3-5; 61:1-3; Matthew 16:6; John 5:8-18)

MARK 3:14,15

Then [Jesus] appointed twelve, that they might be with Him and that He might send them out to preach, and to have power to heal sicknesses and to cast out demons.

~ *PRAYER* ~

Father, I thank You for the authority that You have given me to heal the sick and cast out demons.

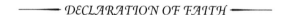

——— *DECLARATION OF FAITH* ———

Jesus has sent me into the world as an ambassador of the kingdom. He has given me power and authority to heal the sick and cast out devils.

(Luke 9:1,2; 10:19; 2 Corinthians 5:18-20; Mark 16:15-20)

MARK 5:22-43

And behold, one of the rulers of the synagogue came, Jairus by name. And when he saw Him, he fell at His feet and begged Him earnestly, saying, "My little daughter lies at the point of death. Come and lay Your hands on her, that she may be healed, and she will live." So Jesus went with him, and a great multitude followed Him and thronged Him. Now a certain woman had a flow of blood for twelve years, and had suffered many things from many physicians. She had spent all that she had and was no better, but rather grew worse. When she heard about Jesus, she came behind Him in the crowd and touched

His garment. For she said, "If only I may touch His clothes, I shall be made well." Immediately the fountain of her blood was dried up, and she felt in her body that she was healed of the affliction. And Jesus, immediately knowing in Himself that power had gone out of Him, turned around in the crowd and said, "Who touched My clothes?" But His disciples said to Him, "You see the multitude thronging You, and You say, 'Who touched Me?'" And He looked around to see her who had done this thing. But the woman, fearing and trembling, knowing what had happened to her, came and fell down before Him and told Him the whole truth. And He said to her, "Daughter, your faith has made you well. Go in peace, and be healed of your affliction." While He was still speaking, some came from the ruler of the synagogue's house who said, "Your daughter is dead. Why trouble the Teacher any further?" As soon as Jesus heard the word that was spoken, He said to the ruler of the synagogue, "Do not be afraid; only believe." And He permitted no one to follow Him except Peter, James, and John the brother of James. Then He came to the house of the ruler of the synagogue, and saw a tumult and those who wept and wailed loudly. When He came in, He said to them, "Why make this commotion and weep? The child is not dead, but sleeping." And they ridiculed Him. But when He had put them all outside, He took the father and the mother of the child, and those who were with Him, and entered where the child was lying. Then He took the child by the hand, and said to her, "Talitha, cumi," which is translated, "Little girl, I say to you, arise." Immediately the girl arose and walked, for she was twelve years of age. And they were overcome with great amazement. But He commanded them strictly that no one should know it, and said that something should be given her to eat.

~ *PRAYER* ~

Father, there are so many truths in these verses. I thank You that I have the Spirit of wisdom and revelation, and that the eyes of my understanding are enlightened. I thank You that You meet me where my faith is, and that my faith will make me well. I thank You that as I purge fear from my life, faith shall remain, and by my faith I can live in health and prosperity. I am not afraid, Father. No matter what I have been told, I hold fast to Your Word as my final authority. I know that You make good on everything You have said. Healing is mine. Prosperity is mine. Peace and security are mine. You, Father, are mine, and I will praise You forever.

———— *DECLARATION OF FAITH* ————

My faith restores me to perfect health when symptoms of sickness come upon me. Jesus has set me free from sickness and has given me His peace.

When I am faced with an evil report in the natural realm, I remain calm and continue to believe. I do not allow fear to rob me of what God has done for me. My faith brings to pass what I need, regardless of what is seen or known in the natural world.

(Numbers 14:1-9; 2 Timothy 1:6,7; Joshua 1:5-9; 2 Corinthians 4:13; 5:7; Hebrews 11:1; Mark 10:52; 11:22-25; Galatians 3:13; Matthew 9:22; Isaiah 53:4,5)

MARK 6:4-6

But Jesus said to them, "A prophet is not without honor except in his own country, among his own relatives, and in his own house." Now He could do no mighty work there, except that He laid His hands on a few sick people and healed them. And He marveled because of their unbelief. Then He went about the villages in a circuit, teaching.

~ PRAYER ~

Father, I see that Jesus' power is limited only by my faith. I will not be as one who does not believe. Only by faith will I be made whole. Therefore, I choose to believe in Your Word. You said it, and that settles it. I am healed, in Jesus' name!

—— DECLARATION OF FAITH ——

I receive from God only what I can acquire by faith. If I fail to exercise my faith, I am telling God to limit His power in my life.

The miracles that follow me as an ambassador of Christ require both my faith and the faith of those who are to receive them. If someone wants what I have, if they believe they receive it, they shall have it.

(Hebrews 11:1,6; Mark 11:22-25; 16:15-20; Matthew 21:19-22; 2 Corinthians 5:18-20)

MARK 6:7,12-13

[Jesus] called the twelve to Himself, and began to send them out two by two, and gave them power over unclean spirits... So they went out and preached that people should repent. And they cast out many demons, and anointed with oil many who were sick, and healed them.

~ PRAYER ~

Father, I thank You for the power that You have given me over unclean spirits. In You I have power to cast out demons and heal the sick.

———— DECLARATION OF FAITH ————

I have power and authority over all unclean spirits and have been commissioned by the Lord to set their captives free.

I have been sent into the world by Him to preach the gospel and teach the Word of repentance.

I drive out all demons from my presence in Jesus' name, and when I anoint the sick with oil, they are healed.

(Luke 9:1,2; 10:18,19; Matthew 28:18-20; James 5:14; Isaiah 61:1-3; Mark 16:15-20)

MARK 6:54-56

When they came out of the boat, immediately the people recognized [Jesus], ran through that whole surrounding region, and began to carry about on beds those who were sick to wherever they heard He was. Wherever He entered, into villages, cities, or the country, they laid the sick in the marketplaces, and begged Him that they might just touch the hem of His garment. And as many as touched Him were made well.

~ PRAYER ~

Father, as many as touched Jesus were made well. How much more shall I be made well with Him living inside of me.

—— DECLARATION OF FAITH ——

I know my Lord and I'm well acquainted with His power. He is the Lord of all health and He dwells within me. I do not need to touch the hem of His garment; I am His body. I am His fullness in this earth as He fills me in every way. Wherever the Lord entered, He brought healing. He has entered me, and His healing is manifested through me.

(Ephesians 1:17-23; Romans 8:11; 1 Corinthians 6:19,20; Matthew 8:3)

MARK 8:22-25

Then [Jesus] came to Bethsaida; and they brought a blind man to Him, and begged Him to touch him. So He took the blind man by the hand and led him out of the town. And when He had spit on his eyes and put His hands on him, He asked him if he saw anything. And he looked up and said, "I see men like trees, walking." Then He put His hands on his eyes again and made him look up. And he was restored and saw everyone clearly.

~ PRAYER ~

Father, I can see that healing isn't always immediately manifested. However, I also see that persistence of faith is necessary to bring forth the complete manifestation of what I am praying for.

Therefore, Father, I completely commit myself to Your Word. I know that You are restoring me to perfect wholeness even as we speak. I will keep on praying and keep on having hands laid on me until my healing is complete.

——— DECLARATION OF FAITH ———

God is more than willing to pour His healing power into my body. It is His absolute will that I be restored to perfect health. Therefore, no matter how long it takes, I will continue to pray until my healing is complete and I stand entirely whole.

(Isaiah 53:3-5; 61:1-3; Matthew 15:31; Mark 4:13-20)

MARK 9:17-29

Then one of the crowd answered and said, "Teacher, I brought You my son, who has a mute spirit. And wherever it seizes him, it throws him down; he foams at the mouth, gnashes his teeth, and becomes rigid. So I spoke to Your disciples, that they should cast it out, but they could not." [Jesus] answered him and said, "O faithless generation, how long shall I be with you? How long shall I bear with you? Bring him to Me." Then they brought him to Him. And when he saw Him, immediately the spirit convulsed him, and he fell on the ground and wallowed, foaming at the mouth. So He asked his father, "How long has this been happening to him?" And he said, "From childhood. And often he has thrown him both into the fire and into the water to destroy him. But if You can do anything, have compassion on us and help us." Jesus said to him, "If you can believe, all things are possible to him who believes." Immediately the father of the child cried out and said with tears, "Lord, I believe; help my unbelief!" When Jesus saw that the people came running together, He rebuked the unclean spirit, saying to it, "Deaf and dumb spirit, I command you, come out of him and enter him no more!" Then the spirit cried out, convulsed him greatly, and came out of him. And he became as one dead, so that many said, "He is dead." But Jesus took him by the hand and lifted him up, and he arose. And when He had come into the house, His disciples asked Him privately, "Why could we not cast it out?" So He said to them, "This kind can come out by nothing but prayer and fasting."

~ PRAYER ~

Father, I know the importance of feeding my spirit continually so that I can remain strong in Your power. Faith comes by revelation knowledge of Your Word. Therefore, I shall meditate in it day and night so that I may prosper and have good success in all that I do. I know that all things are possible for me as long as I can believe. Feed me, Father. Feed my faith as I pour Your Word into my mind, body, and spirit. Partner with me as I cast the devil from my life in Jesus' name, and advance Your kingdom in this earth.

—— DECLARATION OF FAITH ——

I believe in God's power and ability within me. Therefore, all things are possible for me.

I have been given authority over spirits who operate with a specific purpose, such as those who render people deaf and mute. In Jesus' name, I have authority to command them to come out of people and never enter them again.

I remain steadfast in my prayer life so that when I come up against a stubborn and obstinate devil, it will pose no problem for me.

(Joshua 1:8; Ephesians 1:17-23; 6:10-18; James 5:16; Luke 9:1,2; 10:19; Mark 1:25; 11:22-25; 16:17-20; Psalm 91:13; Colossians 1:29; Philippians 2:13; Matthew 21:19-22)

MARK 10:46-52

Now they came to Jericho. As He went out of Jericho with His disciples and a great multitude, blind Bartimaeus, the son of Timaeus, sat by the road begging. And when he heard that it was Jesus of Nazareth, he began to cry out and say, "Jesus, Son of David, have mercy on me!" Then many warned him to be quiet; but he cried out all the more, "Son of David, have mercy on me!" So Jesus stood still and commanded him to be called. Then they called the blind man, saying to him, "Be of good cheer. Rise, He is calling you." And throwing aside his garment, he rose and came to Jesus. So Jesus answered and said to him, "What do you want Me to do for you?" The blind man said to Him, "Rabboni, that I may receive my sight." Then Jesus said to him, "Go your way; your faith has made you well." And immediately he received his sight and followed Jesus on the road.

~ *PRAYER* ~

Father, because of Your great love for me, I have no beggarly garment. I am not a beggar at Your throne; I am a son/daughter! You pour out

Your mercy on me in abundance. All I have to do is ask and You give me the desires of my heart. I don't care what anyone thinks of it, Lord. I only care what You think. I choose to believe Your Word and walk in Your ways. My faith has made me well!

―――――― *DECLARATION OF FAITH* ――――――

I am bold to speak to my heavenly Father about my needs and desires. I know that He is more than willing to entertain my prayers and fulfill all of my requests. I am not a beggar at His throne. I am a son/daughter and an heir to the kingdom. Therefore, I have a right to ask and receive that my joy might be made full.

I know that Jesus paid the price for my healing. Therefore, I receive it by faith, even before the symptoms leave. By faith, my healing is an ever-present fact.

(Matthew 9:22; Mark 5:34; Hebrews 11:1; 2 Corinthians 4:13; 5:7; 1 Peter 2:24; John 16:23,24)

MARK 11:22-26

So Jesus answered and said to them, "Have faith in God. For assuredly, I say to you, whoever says to this mountain, 'Be removed and be cast into the sea,' and does not doubt in his heart, but believes that those things he says will be done, he will have whatever he says. Therefore I say to you, whatever things you ask when you pray, believe that you receive them, and you will have them. And whenever you stand praying, if you have anything against anyone, forgive him, that your

Father in heaven may also forgive you your trespasses. But if you do not forgive, neither will your Father in heaven forgive your trespasses."

~ *PRAYER* ~

Father, You have clearly taught me the power of my words. The very spirit of faith is to believe and speak. Therefore, I speak to the mountain of my circumstances and command it to get in line with Your Word. I believe that I have received my healing, Father. It is in me at this very moment. Regardless of how I feel, I am healed.

Body, I speak to you now and command you to be made whole. You work perfectly as God intended. You shall not permit sickness or disease to dwell in you. You are divinely protected from sickness and disease. Healing, flow through me in abundance. Give strength to every cell of my body. Body, you are healed in Jesus' name!

Father, I thank You that You have taken my words and caused them to come to pass.

———— DECLARATION OF FAITH ————

I am constantly functioning in God-like faith.

God has created me as a faith being. My words bring into existence whatever I am believing for that's in line with His Word.

If I command a mountain (a formidable circumstance or barrier) to be removed and cast into the sea, and have no doubt that it will happen, it will happen.

Everything that I believe with my heart and speak from my mouth, within the boundaries of God's Word, becomes reality for me.

Whatever I ask for in prayer, if I believe I have received it, I will have it.

I understand that unforgiveness and strife bring cancellation to what I am praying for. Therefore, I refuse to harbor them in my life. I continually remember my own frame, all that God has forgiven me of, and that I have no right to withhold grace from others when I myself walk in it so freely.

(2 Corinthians 4:13; 5:7; Romans 5:1,2; 10:8-10; Hebrews 11:1,6; Matthew 6:14; 8:13; 17:20; 18:23-35; 21:21,22; Proverbs 18:20,21; Luke 11:9; John 14:13,14; 15:7; 16:23,24; James 1:6-8; 3:2; Ephesians 4:32; Colossians 3:13)

MARK 16:14-20

Later [Jesus] appeared to the eleven as they sat at the table; and He rebuked their unbelief and hardness of heart, because they did not believe those who had seen Him after He had risen. And He said to them, "Go into all the world and preach the gospel to every creature. He who believes and is baptized will be saved; but he who does not believe will be condemned. And these signs will follow those who believe: In My name they will cast out demons; they will speak with new tongues; they will take up serpents; and if they drink anything deadly, it will by no means hurt them; they will lay hands on the sick, and they will recover." So then, after the Lord had spoken to them, He was received up into heaven, and sat down at the right hand of God. And they went out and preached everywhere, the Lord working with them and confirming the word through the accompanying signs. Amen.

~ *PRAYER* ~

Father, I purpose in my heart to believe Your Word without reservation. I know that belief is the foundation of my faith, and that without faith it is impossible to please You. As I advance Your kingdom, my faith shall go before me. I will cast out demons, speak with new tongues, and trample on serpents. If I drink any deadly thing it shall not harm me,[1] and when I lay my hands on the sick, the sick shall recover. Father, I thank You that You are my partner. You work with me and confirm Your Word with signs following.

———— *DECLARATION OF FAITH* ————

I have been commissioned to proclaim the gospel to everyone I come in contact with. Those who believe and are baptized shall be saved, but those who do not believe shall remain in condemnation.

As I walk in faith, these signs accompany me:

In Jesus name, I cast out demons,

I speak in tongues.

If needs be, I take up vipers without being harmed.[2]

If I drink any deadly thing,[3] it shall not harm me,

and when I lay my hands on the sick, they recover.

Jesus, my Lord, brother, intercessor, and high priest of my confession, is now seated at the right hand of God the Father, the Majesty on high, and He has bid me to take my place at His side. As I go out to proclaim the Good News, He is working with me, confirming the Word through the signs, wonders, and miracles that accompany me.

(Isaiah 61:1-3; Matthew 28:18-20; Colossians 1:23; 2 Corinthians 5:18-20; John 3:18,36; Acts 2:4; 5:12; Luke 9:1,2; 10:17-19; 1 Corinthians 14:5; James 5:14-16; Psalm 91:10-13; Hebrews 2:11; 1:3; Ephesians 2:6)

CHAPTER EIGHTEEN

LUKE

LUKE 1:37,38,45

"You will conceive in your womb and bring forth a Son, and shall call His name JESUS.... For with God nothing will be impossible." Then Mary said, "Behold the maidservant of the Lord! Let it be to me according to your word." And the angel departed from her. "...Blessed is she who believed, for there will be a fulfillment of those things which were told her from the Lord."

~ PRAYER ~

Father, Mary has shown us a fine example of how to respond to Your Word. There was nothing in her circumstances to show that what the angel said would come to pass. But, she believed anyway. Father, nothing is impossible for You. You have said that I am healed. Therefore, be it unto me according to Your Word! Let there be a fulfillment of those things which You have told me.

—— *DECLARATION OF FAITH* ——

Like Mary, God has set me apart as one who is unique and special.

He makes His declaration to all that I am one of His favored ones and that He is with me in all that I do.

I have no reason to fear, for I have found favor with God.

With God, the Greater One who is within me, nothing is impossible. Every promise that He has given me has within it the power of fulfillment. Therefore, what He says that I am, that is what I am; and, what He says I can do, that is what I can do. All that His Word declares about me is fulfilled as I take hold of it in faith and put it into operation in my life.

I am blessed (happy, joyful, and to be envied) because I believe that I am who God says I am, and I can do what He says I can do.

(Isaiah 43:1-7; 55:11; Hebrews 10:14-17; 11:1-6; 13:5,6; Matthew 17:20; 28:20; Psalms 103:13; 119:138; Job 1:8; Romans 2:11; Joshua 1:5-9; 2 Timothy 1:6,7; Proverbs 11:27; 1 John 4:4; James 1:22; John 14:12)

LUKE 4:17-27

[Jesus] was handed the book of the prophet Isaiah. And when He had opened the book, He found the place where it was written: "The Spirit of the LORD is upon Me, because He has anointed Me to preach the gospel to the poor; He has sent Me to heal the brokenhearted, to proclaim liberty to the captives and recovery of sight to the blind, to set at liberty those who are oppressed; to proclaim the acceptable year of the LORD." Then He closed the book, and gave it back to the attendant and sat down. And the eyes of all who were in the synagogue were fixed on Him. And He began to say to them, "Today this Scripture is fulfilled in your hearing." So all bore witness to Him, and marveled at the gracious words which proceeded out of His mouth. And they said, "Is this not Joseph's son?" He said to them, "You will surely say this proverb to Me, 'Physician, heal yourself! Whatever we have heard done in Capernaum, do also here in Your country.'" Then He said, "Assuredly, I say to you, no prophet is accepted in his own country. But I tell you truly, many widows were in Israel in the days of Elijah, when the heaven was shut up three years and six months, and there was a great famine throughout all the land; but to none of them was Elijah sent except to Zarephath, in the region of Sidon, to a woman who was a widow. And many lepers were in Israel in the time of Elisha the prophet, and none of them was cleansed except Naaman the Syrian."

~ PRAYER ~

Father, I see the admonition in these verses. I am not about to reason against Your promises. I know that Your healing power is available to all, but it will be manifested only for those who will receive it by faith. Therefore, I make my unwavering choice to believe Your Word. I do not look to circumstances or some sign or wonder before I will believe. I look to the Word. That is where my healing is found. I believe it without reservation and I fully expect its manifestation in my life.

──────── *DECLARATION OF FAITH* ────────

I have become one with Jesus and am fully identified with Him in every way.

Like Him, the Spirit of the Lord has come upon me and has anointed me with burden-removing, yoke-destroying power.

I preach the Good News to the poor, declaring freedom from poverty.

I announce deliverance to the captives and recovery of sight to the blind.

I send forth as delivered those who are oppressed and wounded by the trials of life.

I proclaim to all that the day of grace has come—that God is not mad at them but is ready to receive them into His family and show them His continual favor both now and forevermore.

(Job 29:7-11,21-25; 1 Corinthians 1:30; 2:6-16; Psalm 45:2; Galatians 4:5,6; John 14:12; 17:20-23; Isaiah 61:1-3; 1 John 2:20; 2 Corinthians 1:3,4; 5:17-21; 8:9; Matthew 11:5; 28:18-20; Romans 5:1,2)

LUKE 4:38-40

Now [Jesus] arose from the synagogue and entered Simon's house. But Simon's wife's mother was sick with a high fever, and they made request of Him concerning her. So He stood over her and rebuked the fever, and it left her. And immediately she arose and served them. When the sun was setting, all those who had any that were sick with various diseases brought them to Him; and He laid His hands on every one of them and healed them.

~ *PRAYER* ~

Father, once again You show me the power of words. If I but speak to the problem, it must come in line with Your will. Therefore, I rebuke fever and all manner of sickness. I take my authority and command them to leave my presence. *[Speak to whatever you are facing and command it to leave in Jesus' name.]*

——— *DECLARATION OF FAITH* ———

Fever is not permitted to remain in my presence. In Jesus' name, I have complete authority to speak to it and command it to leave, and it absolutely must obey me.

In Jesus, I have been delivered from every disease. In His name, I have the power and ability to bring healing to the bodies of those on whom I lay my hands.

(Mark 11:22-25; 16:18; Philippians 2:10; Isaiah 53:4,5; Matthew 8:17; Galatians 3:13; Luke 10:19)

LUKE 5:12,13

It happened when He was in a certain city, that behold, a man who was full of leprosy saw Jesus; and he fell on his face and implored Him, saying, "Lord, if You are willing, You can make me clean." Then He put out His hand and touched him, saying, "I am willing; be cleansed." Immediately the leprosy left him. And He charged him to tell no one, "But go and show yourself to the priest, and make an offering for your cleansing, as a testimony to them, just as Moses commanded." However, the report went around concerning Him all the more; and great multitudes came together to hear, and to be healed by Him of their infirmities. So He Himself often withdrew into the wilderness and prayed.

~ PRAYER ~

Father, Your heart is so evident in Your Word. How can we ever doubt Your love or Your willingness to heal us? As for me, Father, I choose to believe. I receive Your healing now. I speak to the healing power within me:

Healing, flow through me mightily. Attack the problem from the root and restore me to perfect health. Body, I command you now, be cleansed of your infirmity, in Jesus' name.

——— DECLARATION OF FAITH ———

Jesus, my Lord, Savior, and Redeemer, is more than willing to provide His healing power for me whenever I need it.

Through Him, I can lay my hands on the sick and command healing to come into their bodies.

I regularly and consistently take the time to go to an isolated place, free of distraction, to pray and fellowship with my heavenly Father.

I am not moved by need, nor do I focus on how much work there is to do. I am moved by design, doing things the way God has commanded.

It is in God's design that I regularly rest and get prayed up, regardless of what needs to be done.

(Mark 1:35; 6:46; 11:23,24; 16:18; Matthew 6:6; Luke 4:42; 9:10; 10:9; Deuteronomy 28:1; Exodus 14:1-15; Isaiah 53:5; Galatians 3:13; James 5:15)

LUKE 5:17-26

Now it happened on a certain day, as [Jesus] was teaching, that there were Pharisees and teachers of the law sitting by, who had come out of every town of Galilee, Judea, and Jerusalem. And the power of the Lord was present to heal them. Then behold, men brought on a bed a man who was paralyzed, whom they sought to bring in and lay before Him. And when they could not find how they might bring him in, because of the crowd, they went up on the housetop and let him down with his bed through the tiling into the midst before Jesus. When He saw their faith, He said to him, "Man, your sins are forgiven you." And the scribes and the Pharisees began to reason, saying, "Who is this who speaks blasphemies? Who can forgive sins but God alone?" But when Jesus perceived their thoughts, He answered and said to them, "Why are you reasoning in your hearts? Which is easier, to say, 'Your sins are forgiven you,' or to say, 'Rise up and walk'? But that you may know that the Son of Man has power on earth to forgive sins"—He said to the man who was paralyzed, "I say to you, arise, take up your bed, and go to your house." Immediately he rose up before them, took up what he had been lying on, and departed to his own house, glorifying God. And they were all amazed, and they glorified God and were filled with fear, saying, "We have seen strange things today!"

~ PRAYER ~

Father, You dwell within me. My body is Your very temple. Therefore, Your healing power is always present with me. You have cleansed me of all sin and healed me of every sickness and disease. Your power restores every failing body part to perfect wellness. My nervous system is now working in perfect harmony with the rest of my body. All paralysis is healed and every internal organ is restored to its maximum potential. It's time for me to get up and get some work done, in Jesus' name!

DECLARATION OF FAITH

I can see when faith has risen in a person's heart, and as a carrier of God's power, I am ever ready to provide the healing that they need.

In Jesus, I have the ability and authority to release an individual from the power of sin and provide healing for any area of their lives.

My words are the carriers of God's power in this earth, and they bring deliverance to those held captive by the forces of darkness.

In Jesus, I am a discerner of the thoughts, questions, and intentions of those who oppose the truth, and I have all the wisdom that I need to handle any situation or confrontation I have with them.

I am a man/woman of faith.

The power of sin has been broken over my life.

I have every right to the healing power that God so longs for me to have, and I will do whatever it takes to receive it into my life.

(Mark 2:8; 11:23,24; Luke 8:43-48; 20:23; James 5:14-16; John 20:22,23; 1 Corinthians 2:6-16; 2 Corinthians 5:20; Galatians 4:5,6)

LUKE 6:17-19

[Jesus] came down with them and stood on a level place with a crowd of His disciples and a great multitude of people from all Judea and Jerusalem, and from the seacoast of Tyre and Sidon, who came to hear Him and be healed of their diseases, as well as those who were tormented with unclean spirits. And they were healed. And the whole multitude sought to touch Him, for power went out from Him and healed them all.

~ *PRAYER* ~

Father, unclean spirits have wreaked havoc in my life for the last time. I thank You that You have put the fear and dread of me on their hearts. I set myself against every one of them:

Devil, I command you to leave my circle of influence. I do not permit you to torment me or my loved ones. You leave now, in Jesus' name.

Father, I thank You that healing power flows through me and pours forth from me. As Your ambassador, I bring healing wherever I go and in whatever I do.

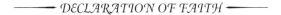

——— *DECLARATION OF FAITH* ———

People are drawn to the Holy Spirit, who is within me, and I respond to their faith by being an avenue of God's healing power for them.

Unclean spirits of every kind flee from my presence and power goes forth from me to meet the needs of the expecting one.

(Job 29:21-25; James 4:7; 5:14-16; Luke 10:19; John 14:12; Mark 16:17-20)

LUKE 7:2-10

A certain centurion's servant, who was dear to him, was sick and ready to die. So when he heard about Jesus, he sent elders of the Jews to Him, pleading with Him to come and heal his servant. And when they came to Jesus, they begged Him earnestly, saying that the one for whom He should do this was deserving, "for he loves our nation, and has built us a synagogue." Then Jesus went with them. And when He was already not far from the house, the centurion sent friends to Him, saying to Him, "Lord, do not trouble Yourself, for I am not worthy that You should enter under my roof. Therefore I did not even think myself worthy to come to You. But say the word, and my servant will be healed. For I also am a man placed under authority, having soldiers under me. And I say to one, 'Go,' and he goes; and to another, 'Come,' and he comes; and to my servant, 'Do this,' and he does it." When Jesus heard these things, He marveled at him, and turned around and said to the crowd that followed Him, "I say to you, I have not found such great faith, not even in Israel!" And those who were sent, returning to the house, found the servant well who had been sick.

~ PRAYER ~

Father, I recognize once again the power of the words that I speak. The spirit of faith is believing and speaking. When I speak Your Word, it charges to the root of the problem and whatever I need is soon manifested. Lord, You have made me a man/woman of authority. When I speak the Word, my circumstances come in line with Your will. When I tell sickness to go, it goes. When I tell healing to come, it comes. The walk of faith that You are teaching me is ever increasingly clear to me, Father. I choose to believe, and the things that I say shall come to pass, in Jesus' name.

─── *DECLARATION OF FAITH* ───

I understand the power that God has placed in His Word. It is the ultimate authority in heaven and earth, and on my lips it brings healing and deliverance to those in need.

(Psalms 107:20; 138:2; Isaiah 42:21)

LUKE 7:20-23

When the men had come to Him, they said, "John the Baptist has sent us to You, saying, 'Are You the Coming One, or do we look for another?'" And that very hour He cured many of infirmities, afflictions, and evil spirits; and to many blind He gave sight. Jesus answered and said to them, "Go and tell John the things you have seen and heard: that the blind see, the lame walk, the lepers are cleansed, the deaf hear, the dead are raised, the poor have the gospel preached to them. And blessed is he who is not offended because of Me."

~ *PRAYER* ~

Father, I stand fast against all reasonings that would cause me to doubt Your power in my life. Jesus is my Savior and Lord. The kingdom of heaven has come unto me, and health and prosperity are in its wake. Healing is an ever-present fact within me. Jesus is my elder brother and I am Your own son/daughter. I am not offended at these things, Father. I am blessed, all that I do prospers, and I remain in good health, in Jesus' name.

———— *DECLARATION OF FAITH* ————

In Jesus, I have come to experience the wonder-working power of God.

His healing power goes with me wherever I go. The blind see, the deaf hear, the lame rise and walk, the dead are raised to life, and the poor are shown the way to an abundance of riches.

Through Jesus, every demon is subject to my authority.

I consider it ludicrous to be offended or resentful at these things, but I take them as the fundamental results of being one with God.

I will never reject the manifestation of the power of God in my life!

(Ephesians 1:17-23; Mark 16:15-20; Isaiah 61:1-3; Luke 10:19; John 17:20-26; 2 Timothy 3:5; 3 John 2)

LUKE 8:41-55

And behold, there came a man named Jairus, and he was a ruler of the synagogue. And he fell down at Jesus' feet and begged Him to come to his house, for he had an only daughter about twelve years of age, and she was dying. But as He went, the multitudes thronged Him. Now a woman, having a flow of blood for twelve years, who had spent all her livelihood on physicians and could not be healed by any, came from behind and touched the border of His garment. And immediately her flow of blood stopped. And Jesus said, "Who touched Me?" When all denied it, Peter and those with him said, "Master, the multitudes throng and press You, and You say, 'Who touched Me?'" But Jesus said, "Somebody touched Me, for I perceived power going out from Me." Now when the woman saw that she was not hidden, she came trembling; and falling down before Him, she declared to Him in the presence of all the people the reason she had touched Him and how she was healed immediately. And He said to her, "Daughter, be of good cheer; your faith has made you well. Go in peace." While He was still speaking, someone came from the ruler of the synagogue's house, saying to him, "Your daughter is dead. Do not trouble the Teacher." But when Jesus heard it, He answered him, saying, "Do not be afraid; only believe, and she will be made well." When He came into the house, He permitted no one to go in except Peter, James, and John, and the father and mother of the girl. Now all wept and mourned for her; but He said, "Do not weep; she is not dead, but sleeping." And they ridiculed Him, knowing that she was dead. But He put them all outside, took her by the hand and called, saying, "Little girl, arise." Then her spirit returned, and she arose immediately. And He commanded that she be given something to eat.

~ *PRAYER* ~

Father, I know that when all earthly hope is gone and the doctors can do no more, my answer is found in You. You are my strength and my shield. You are my deliverance from every trouble and the surety that it will go well with me and I will live a long, full and satisfying life. I am of good cheer, Father. I know that my faith has made me well. I am not afraid. No matter what has been said, I choose to believe. Thank You for my healing, Father. I believe I receive it, in Jesus' name.

———— DECLARATION OF FAITH ————

In Jesus, I have a keen perception of the workings of the power of God in my life. I can sense when the power of God has been poured into a child of faith. I have a thorough understanding of the workings of faith and that it is by faith that we are made well and are able to enter into the peace that supersedes all worldly understanding.

I am never seized with alarm or struck by fear when a bad report comes. I believe in the power and ability of God within me, and I am confident that He will cause me to triumph in any situation.

(Joshua 1:5-9; 2 Corinthians 2:14; Colossians 1:29; Ephesians 1:17-23; 3:20; 1 Peter 5:5-7; Hebrews 11:1,6; James 5:16; Mark 5:30; Philippians 4:7)

LUKE 9:1-6

Then [Jesus] called His twelve disciples together and gave them power and authority over all demons, and to cure diseases. He sent them to preach the kingdom of God and to heal the sick. And He said to them, "Take nothing for the journey, neither staffs nor bag nor bread nor money; and do not have two tunics apiece. Whatever house you enter, stay there, and from there depart. And whoever will not receive you, when you go out of that city, shake off the very dust from your feet as a testimony against them." So they departed and went through the towns, preaching the gospel and healing everywhere.

~ PRAYER ~

Father, I thank You that I have power and authority over all of the power and authority of the enemy. You have given me the anointing to cast out demons and cure diseases. This gospel of Your kingdom encompasses every kind of healing. Teach me to operate in this anointing, Father. Help me to walk in the wisdom I have been given.

———— DECLARATION OF FAITH ————

Jesus has given me power and authority over all demons and to cure sicknesses and diseases of every kind. He has sent me out to proclaim the present fact of the kingdom of God and to bring healing to a hurting world.

I have been sent into the neighborhoods of my city and from town to town to proclaim the gospel and restore health to the afflicted everywhere.

(Acts 1:8; Mark 16:15-20; Isaiah 61:1-3; Matthew 28:18-20; 2 Corinthians 5:18-20; Luke 10:19)

LUKE 9:11

But when the multitudes knew it, they followed [Jesus]; and He received them and spoke to them about the kingdom of God, and healed those who had need of healing.

~ *PRAYER* ~

Father, I thank You that You meet my every need. I have the kingdom within me and it is full of Your healing power. I will walk in this light and live out my healing, in Jesus' name.

———— DECLARATION OF FAITH ————

I welcome all who are willing to listen to the message of the gospel—bringing the present fact of the kingdom of God into their midst, chasing off Satan and his demons, and restoring health to the oppressed and afflicted.

(Philippians 2:12,13; Mark 16:15-20; Luke 10:19; Isaiah 61:1-3)

LUKE 10:1-11

After these things the Lord appointed seventy others also, and sent them two by two before His face into every city and place where He Himself was about to go. Then He said to them, "The harvest truly is great, but the laborers are few; therefore pray the Lord of the harvest to send out laborers into His harvest. Go your way; behold, I send you out as lambs among wolves. Carry neither money bag, knapsack, nor sandals; and greet no one along the road. But whatever house you enter, first say, 'Peace to this house.' And if a son of peace is there, your peace will rest on it; if not, it will return to you. And remain in the same house, eating and drinking such things as they give, for the laborer is worthy of his wages. Do not go from house to house. Whatever city you enter, and they receive you, eat such things as are set before you. And heal the sick there, and say to them, 'The kingdom of God has come near to you.' But whatever city you enter, and they do not receive you, go out into its streets and say, 'The very dust of your city which clings to us we wipe off against you. Nevertheless know this, that the kingdom of God has come near you.'"

~ PRAYER ~

Father, I recognize that I have been made an ambassador of Your kingdom. I am a carrier of Your healing power to the world. Jesus is within me, and His anointing flows through me. If I run into opposition, where people are offended at Your blessings, I'll simply shake the dust off my feet and go to those who want to receive. I'm not going to fret over this in any way, Father. I'm just going to walk with You and get the job done, in Jesus' name.

——— *DECLARATION OF FAITH* ———

I pray for the Lord of the Harvest to send laborers into the harvest fields to bring the lost to salvation.

Whenever I bring God's healing power to the sick, I explain to them that it is the kingdom of God that has entered their presence and His power alone has healed them.

(Mark 3:15; 16:15-20; Matthew 3:2; 9:37,38; John 4:35; 2 Thessalonians 3:1)

LUKE 10:17-20

Then the seventy returned with joy, saying, "Lord, even the demons are subject to us in Your name." And He said to them, "I saw Satan fall like lightning from heaven. Behold, I give you the authority to trample on serpents and scorpions, and over all the power of the enemy, and nothing shall by any means hurt you. Nevertheless do not rejoice in this, that the spirits are subject to you, but rather rejoice because your names are written in heaven."

~ *PRAYER* ~

Father, I thank You that I am in Jesus. In Him I live and move and have my being. The very works that He did, I do. The demons were subject unto Him, and now they are subject unto me. They could not hurt Him, and neither can they hurt me. I carry with me His very authority and I will put that authority to work. Nevertheless, Father, I do not rejoice in my authority over the devil. He is not that important. My joy is in the fact that I am Your son/daughter and my name is written in heaven.

———— *DECLARATION OF FAITH* ————

All wicked spirits are subject to my authority in Jesus' name.

I have all of the authority that I need to trample down serpents and scorpions, and I have mental, physical, and spiritual strength over and above all that the enemy possesses. There is nothing that Satan can do to harm me in any way.

For me, Satan and his demons are little more than harmless, pesky bugs.

Nevertheless, I do not find great joy in my ability to cast out demons, or the fact that they are subject to my authority, but I rejoice that my name has been written in heaven and that I am honored as a son/daughter of the living God.

(John 14:10-14; Mark 16:17,18; Luke 9:1,2; Psalm 91:13; Ephesians 1:17-23; Philippians 4:3)

LUKE 13:10-17

Now He was teaching in one of the synagogues on the Sabbath. And behold, there was a woman who had a spirit of infirmity eighteen years, and was bent over and could in no way raise herself up. But when Jesus saw her, He called her to Him and said to her, "Woman, you are loosed from your infirmity." And He laid His hands on her, and immediately she was made straight, and glorified God. But the ruler of the synagogue answered with indignation, because Jesus had healed on the Sabbath; and he said to the crowd, "There are six days on which men ought to work; therefore come and be healed on them, and not on the Sabbath day." The Lord then answered him and said, "Hypocrite! Does not each one of you on the Sabbath loose his ox or donkey from the stall, and lead it away to water it? So ought not this woman, being a daughter of Abraham, whom Satan has bound—think of it—for eighteen years, be loosed from this bond on the Sabbath?" And when He said these things, all His adversaries were put to shame; and all the multitude rejoiced for all the glorious things that were done by Him.

~ PRAYER ~

Father, I recognize that I have the keys of the kingdom. Therefore, I loose myself from all infirmity. I know by Your Word that You receive glory, honor, and praise when I receive my healing and live free of Satan's bondage. I will not sit under a poisonous ministry that denies my right to receive what You have clearly given me. I choose to plant myself in good ground. I am not a slave of the devil, and I will not allow religious hypocrites to keep me in bondage. I am free in Christ Jesus!

—— DECLARATION OF FAITH ——

I fully understand that sickness is of the devil and that his authority has been thoroughly stripped from my life. I have been set free from the power of sin and sickness!

I give due recognition to God's healing power in my life, and I do not fail to remember Him and give Him praise for what He has done.

I am a covenant partner with the Lord of the universe. As a provision of the covenant, I have been set free from all of Satan's power and authority.

Everyone who chooses to make themselves my enemy shall be put to shame. I am a man/woman of unquestionable honor and integrity, and people continually give God glory for the things He is doing in my life.

(Acts 9:17; 10:38; Colossians 1:13; 2:15; Romans 6:14,18; 1 Peter 2:24; James 5:14,15; Psalms 79:12; 103:1-5; Hebrews 8:6; 10:15-17; Luke 10:17-19; Isaiah 54:17; Proverbs 11:8; Deuteronomy 28:7,9,10; Mark 5:19,20)

LUKE 13:18-21

Then [Jesus] said, "What is the kingdom of God like? And to what shall I compare it? It is like a mustard seed, which a man took and put in his garden; and it grew and became a large tree, and the birds of the air nested in its branches." And again He said, "To what shall I liken the kingdom of God? It is like leaven, which a woman took and hid in three measures of meal till it was all leavened."

~ PRAYER ~

Father, I know that it is by faith and patience that I receive Your promises. I recognize that I must sow kingdom principles and allow them to grow and weed out all of the other garbage that has been sown into my life through the years. I know that Your healing power is working within me at this very moment. With the words that I speak, I energize that healing power and in time there will not be a single trace of any sickness, disease, or infirmity in my life.

—— DECLARATION OF FAITH ——

I operate the principles of the kingdom in the spirit of faith that has been given to me. I understand that when I sow these principles into my life, they are like grains of mustard seed. Though they are small in comparison to all of the other seeds that have been sown in me, through faith and patience I can water them until their roots have choked out everything else and all that is left is the God-kind of life. In this manner, I receive such an abundance of blessings that I have all that I need and plenty left over. I declare that my life is a refuge to everyone in my circle of influence.

I operate the principles of the kingdom faithfully. They are like the tiny bit of yeast that it takes to make the bread rise. When I put them into operation, it does not look like anything is happening. But I know that, in time, the yeast of God's kingdom principles will infiltrate the whole lump (every issue of my life) until every part of the lump is saturated and controlled by it.

(Galatians 6:9; 2 Corinthians 4:13; 9:5-11; Hebrews 6:12; Matthew 13:31-33; Genesis 12:3)

LUKE 13:31,32

On that very day some Pharisees came, saying to [Jesus], "Get out and depart from here, for Herod wants to kill You." And He said to them, "Go, tell that fox, 'Behold, I cast out demons and perform cures today and tomorrow, and the third day I shall be perfected.'"

~ *PRAYER* ~

Father, what a glorious day that third day was! At that moment, Jesus had fulfilled all that He needed to do in order to give me what I now enjoy. Now the devil not only has to deal with Jesus, he has to deal with me as well. Father, I am awed that I am in Christ Jesus. I'm in the Anointed One and the Anointed One is in me! I can now do the very things that He did, and even greater works can I do because He has gone on to You. I'm stepping out in faith, Father. I'm going to get some folks healed, in Jesus' name!

———— DECLARATION OF FAITH ————

Jesus has finished His course and has taken His seat at the right hand of the Majesty on high—God the Father. I, along with my other brothers and sisters in Christ, have taken over His work in the earth. Because of the power of attorney that Jesus has given me to use His holy name, I regularly drive out demons, perform healings, and set the captives free.

(John 14:12; Hebrews 1:3; Acts 1:8; Mark 16:15-20; Matthew 28:18-20; Ephesians 1:17-23; 2:6)

LUKE 14:1-4

Now it happened, as He went into the house of one of the rulers of the Pharisees to eat bread on the Sabbath, that they watched Him closely. And behold, there was a certain man before Him who had dropsy. And Jesus, answering, spoke to the lawyers and Pharisees, saying, "Is it lawful to heal on the Sabbath?" But they kept silent. And He took him and healed him, and let him go.

~ PRAYER ~

Thank You, Father, for the revelation that healing is proper anytime, anywhere, and under any conditions. You want me well, and Your healing is available to me no matter where I am or what I am doing.

——— DECLARATION OF FAITH ———

I am healed of any dropsied condition that would dare attach itself to me. I do not retain water in unhealthy ways. My body works perfectly and water is released from my system in perfect timing, in Jesus' name.

(Mark 2:27,28; 3:1-5; Luke 13:10-16; Deuteronomy 28:15-68)

LUKE 17:12-21

Then as He entered a certain village, there met Him ten men who were lepers, who stood afar off. And they lifted up their voices and said, "Jesus, Master, have mercy on us!" So when He saw them, He said to them, "Go, show yourselves to the priests." And so it was that as they went, they were cleansed. And one of them, when he saw that he was healed, returned, and with a loud voice glorified God, and fell down on his face at His feet, giving Him thanks. And he was a Samaritan. So Jesus answered and said, "Were there not ten cleansed? But where are the nine? Were there not any found who returned to give glory to God except this foreigner?" And He said to him, "Arise, go your way. Your faith has made you well." Now when He was asked by the Pharisees when the kingdom of God would come, He answered them and said, "The kingdom of God does not come with observation; nor will they say, 'See here!' or 'See there!' For indeed, the kingdom of God is within you."

~ *PRAYER* ~

Father, I see in these verses that the manifestation of healing did not come until the lepers responded to the Word. That's faith. Father, open the eyes of my understanding so I can clearly perceive this. I know that my faith makes me well, in spite of what my situation looks like. You went on to say that the kingdom is within me. That means that Your healing is within me. Therefore, Father, by faith I receive the manifestation of Your healing power. It is in me, and it is flowing through me, in Jesus' name.

———— DECLARATION OF FAITH ————

My faith restores me to perfect health. I can get up and go about my business this day free of all sickness.

The kingdom of God is not something that is coming one day with great signs or a visible display of majesty. No one is going to say, "Look, here is the kingdom!" or "Look up in the clouds; the kingdom is coming!"

The kingdom of God is already here. It is within me and all around me.

(Matthew 4:17; 6:33; 9:22; 11:12; 12:28; 13:31-33; 16:19; Luke 7:50; 8:48; 17:23; 18:42; Hebrews 11:1; 2 Corinthians 4:13; Romans 14:17)

LUKE 18:35-43

Then it happened, as He was coming near Jericho, that a certain blind man sat by the road begging. And hearing a multitude passing by, he asked what it meant. So they told him that Jesus of Nazareth was passing by. And he cried out, saying, "Jesus, Son of David, have mercy on me!" Then those who went before warned him that he should be quiet; but he cried out all the more, "Son of David, have mercy on me!" So Jesus stood still and commanded him to be brought to Him. And when he had come near, He asked him, saying, "What do you want Me to do for you?" He said, "Lord, that I may receive my sight." Then Jesus said to him, "Receive your sight; your faith has made you well." And immediately he received his sight, and followed Him, glorifying God. And all the people, when they saw it, gave praise to God.

~ *PRAYER* ~

Father, I don't care what anyone else thinks. I'm going to do whatever it takes to get my healing. I know that it is Your perfect will that I be made well. You want me to see perfectly, hear perfectly, speak perfectly, and live in absolute perfect health. Therefore, right now I believe I receive my healing. I know, by the authority of Your Word, that my faith has made me well, in Jesus' name.

———— *DECLARATION OF FAITH* ————

I know where the Source of life's power is and I recognize my total and complete dependency upon Him in every way. Without His mercy and grace, I am nothing.

Therefore, I will call upon the Lord in total dependence and confidence in His mercy. I draw near to Him in respect, calling on His name and receiving by faith those specific things that are provided for me in our covenant.

(Ephesians 1:17-23; James 4:6-10; Psalms 16:2; 91:1,2,15; Deuteronomy 28:1-14)

LUKE 22:49-51

When those around [Jesus] saw what was going to happen, they said to Him, "Lord, shall we strike with the sword?" And one of them struck the servant of the high priest and cut off his right ear. But Jesus answered and said, "Permit even this." And He touched his ear and healed him.

~ *PRAYER* ~

Father, Your heart is love itself. Even in the midst of absolute persecution and impertinence, You respond in love. Teach me to do the same, Father. Help me to be just like You.

DECLARATION OF FAITH

No matter what it is that I have done, God will not withhold His healing power from me. I live in the shade of His grace and mercy, and His healing is always available to me to receive by faith.

(Romans 4:5; Galatians 3:1-5; 5:6)

CHAPTER NINETEEN

JOHN

JOHN 4:46-53

So Jesus came again to Cana of Galilee where He had made the water wine. And there was a certain nobleman whose son was sick at Capernaum. When he heard that Jesus had come out of Judea into Galilee, he went to Him and implored Him to come down and heal his son, for he was at the point of death. Then Jesus said to him, "Unless you people see signs and wonders, you will by no means believe." The nobleman said to Him, "Sir, come down before my child dies!" Jesus said to him, "Go your way; your son lives." So the man believed the word that Jesus spoke to him, and he went his way. And as he was now going down, his servants met him and told him, saying, "Your son lives!" Then he inquired of them the hour when he got better. And they said to him, "Yesterday at the seventh hour the fever left him." So the father knew that it was at the same hour in which Jesus said to him, "Your son lives." And he himself believed, and his whole household.

~ *PRAYER* ~

Father, I have committed myself to believe in spite of any signs or wonders. I believe Your Word, not my circumstances. You are God Almighty. What a fool I would be if I chose not to believe You. No, Father, I will believe no matter what I see or feel. Your Word is truth and I will not turn from it.

———— *DECLARATION OF FAITH* ————

The Word of the Lord has been given, and I believe it without exception, compromise, or wavering. It is settled and accomplished in my life.

(James 1:6-8; Isaiah 55:11; Psalms 107:20; 119:89-93)

JOHN 5:1-17

After this there was a feast of the Jews, and Jesus went up to Jerusalem. Now there is in Jerusalem by the Sheep Gate a pool, which is called in Hebrew, Bethesda, having five porches. In these lay a great multitude of sick people, blind, lame, paralyzed, waiting for the moving of the water. For an angel went down at a certain time into the pool and stirred up the water; then whoever stepped in first, after the stirring of the water, was made well of whatever disease he had. Now a certain man was there who had an infirmity thirty-eight years. When Jesus saw him lying there, and knew that he already had been in that condition a long time, He said to him, "Do you want to be made well?" The sick man answered Him, "Sir, I have no man to put me into the pool when the water is stirred up; but while I am coming, another steps down before me." Jesus said to him, "Rise, take up your bed and walk." And immediately the man was made well, took up his bed, and walked. And that day was the Sabbath. The Jews therefore said to him who was cured, "It is the Sabbath; it is not lawful for you to carry your bed." He answered them, "He who made me well said to me, 'Take up your bed and walk.'" Then they asked him, "Who is the Man who said to you, 'Take up your bed and walk'?" But the one who was healed did not know who it was, for Jesus had withdrawn, a multitude being in that place. Afterward Jesus found him in the temple, and said to him, "See, you have been made well. Sin no more, lest a worse thing come upon you." The man departed and told the Jews that it was Jesus who had made him well. For this reason the Jews persecuted Jesus, and sought to kill Him, because He had done these things on the Sabbath. But Jesus answered them, "My Father has been working until now, and I have been working."

~ PRAYER ~

Father, I thank You that I don't have to concern myself with something like waiting for a stirring of the water, or whether there is someone who can help me in. I am healed in spite of any stirring, and in spite of the absence of any person to help me get my healing. I am healed by the stripes of Jesus, not by relying on others. It is by His Word alone that I stand completely whole.

———— *DECLARATION OF FAITH* ————

In Jesus, I have been made well. I will not dishonor Him by continuing in sin, thus leaving the door opened for the devil to attack me with another wave of his foul sicknesses.

My heavenly Father has never ceased to do His work. Even today He is performing mighty miracles in this world, and He has honored me with the privilege of working together with Him.

(Isaiah 53:4,5; 1 Peter 2:24; Matthew 8:17; James 4:7,8; 5:14-16; Philippians 2:13; Colossians 1:29; Mark 16:20; Hebrews 13:8)

JOHN 9:1-7

Now as Jesus passed by, He saw a man who was blind from birth. And His disciples asked Him, saying, "Rabbi, who sinned, this man or his parents, that he was born blind?" Jesus answered, "Neither this man nor his parents sinned, but that the works of God should be revealed in him. I must work the works of Him who sent Me while it is day; the night is coming when no one can work. As long as I am in the world, I am the light of the world." When He had said these things, He spat on the ground and made clay with the saliva; and He anointed the eyes of the blind man with the clay. And He said to him, "Go, wash in the pool of Siloam" (which is translated, Sent). So he went and washed, and came back seeing.

~ PRAYER ~

Thank You, Father, for revealing to me that there are no ailments that I simply have to accept in my life. Just because I was born with something doesn't mean that I have to live with it. I also thank You that I don't have to concern myself with the reasons why I have ended up in the condition I am in. You are not concerned with it, and neither am I. Your only concern is that I repent and receive my healing by faith. Therefore, Father, I say in harmony with Your Word that I am healed. I have my healing in spite of any human logic that would tell me that I don't deserve it, or that You don't want me to have it. I know Your Word, Father. I have read it in the many passages of this book. You are clearly willing to make me whole. In fact, You have promised that by Jesus' stripes I already am healed. This is Your Word, Father, and I choose to walk in it.

--- DECLARATION OF FAITH ---

The reasons for the ailments in people's lives are not my chief concern. What I am concerned with is seeing them healed and setting them free.

I am continually about my Father's business—doing the work of Jesus in this earth. In Jesus, I have become the light of the world, and it is both my privilege and my duty to continue His work.

(Isaiah 61:1-3; 2 Corinthians 5:18-20; Mark 16:15-20; Matthew 28:18-20; John 1:5,9; 14:12; 17:6-26)

JOHN 12:37-41

But although [Jesus] had done so many signs before them, they did not believe in Him, that the word of Isaiah the prophet might be fulfilled, which he spoke: "Lord, who has believed our report? And to whom has the arm of the LORD been revealed?" Therefore they could not believe, because Isaiah said again: "He has blinded their eyes and hardened their hearts, lest they should see with their eyes, lest they should understand with their hearts and turn, so that I should heal them." These things Isaiah said when he saw His glory and spoke of Him.

~ PRAYER ~

Father, I believe Your report. I understand what Jesus has done for me and I choose to walk in it. You have provided my healing. Therefore, I am healed.

──── DECLARATION OF FAITH ────

I have believed the report of the Word. The arm of the Lord has been revealed to me, and I have not hardened my heart against it. I see with my spiritual eyes and understand with my heart. I have turned to the Lord, and He has faithfully healed me in accordance with His Word.

(Isaiah 6:10; 53:1-5; 1 Peter 2:24; Matthew 8:16,17)

JOHN 14:12-14

"Most assuredly, I say to you, he who believes in Me, the works that I do he will do also; and greater works than these he will do, because I go to My Father. And whatever you ask in My name, that I will do, that the Father may be glorified in the Son. If you ask anything in My name, I will do it.

~ PRAYER ~

Father, I believe in Jesus and have received Him as my Lord and Savior. I am now one with Him in all things. The Anointed One and His anointing are in me, and I am in Him. Through Him, I do the very same kinds of things that He did. I know that whatever I ask You in His name, He will do so that You may receive glory. I am fixed in my faith, Lord. Through Your Word I can see exactly how Jesus lived. He spoke words of faith to His circumstances and His circumstances lined up with Your will. Therefore, I will speak to my own circumstances so that my life also is lived in harmony with Your will. I am determined, Father, that through me You shall receive abundance of glory.

———— DECLARATION OF FAITH ————

Through Jesus, I am fully capable of doing the very same things that He did in His earth walk. He has even made me able to do greater things than He did, because He has risen and gone on to the Father.

Jesus himself, through His name, brings to pass whatever I command in this natural world. Everything outside of His will must bow to His authority.

Whatever I ask for, in His name, I receive so that the Father may be glorified through the Son. Only through Jesus are my prayers answered. He has given me the very power of attorney to use His name.

It is like a legal document proclaiming that all of the power that is in His name is now mine to use. I can freely draw upon all that He is and all that He has. Whatever I have asked for in His name, I can confidently claim as done.

(John 15:7; 16:23,24; 17:20-26; Mark 11:22-25; 16:15-20; Matthew 28:18-20; 2 Corinthians 5:17-21; Acts 1:8; 2:43; 4:23-33; 1 Peter 1:2-4; Colossians 1:29; Ephesians 1:17-23; Hebrews 10:14; 1 John 5:14,15; Philippians 2:10)

JOHN 16:23,24

"In that day you will ask Me nothing. Most assuredly, I say to you, whatever you ask the Father in My name He will give you. Until now you have asked nothing in My name. Ask, and you will receive, that your joy may be full."

~ *PRAYER* ~

Father, I ask and receive that my joy may be full. I am fully aware of the access to You that Jesus bought for me. I come boldly before You, Father. I know that You receive me on the basis of Jesus and not my own works. Your Word and Your will are manifested in Jesus. And because Your Word is strong in me, I know that I can ask You for anything that I want that's in line with Your Word and You will grant it.

—— *DECLARATION OF FAITH* ——

My heart rejoices in Jesus, and no one can take my joy from me.

I am now a born-again child of God—the very brother/sister of Jesus himself.

In His name, I have all that I desire from God. My heavenly Father freely grants me whatever I desire that is in accordance with His will and purpose as established in His Word. What I ask for in Jesus' name is a done deal the moment I ask. Therefore, I will continually ask, receiving all that I desire from God, so that my joy may be made complete.

(Nehemiah 8:10; 1 Peter 1:8; John 3:3; 14:13,14; 15:7,11; 17:13;
2 Corinthians 5:17; Titus 3:5; Hebrews 2:11; Romans 8:28-30; Matthew 7:7;
1 John 5:14,15)

CHAPTER TWENTY

ACTS

ACTS 3:1-16

Now Peter and John went up together to the temple at the hour of prayer, the ninth hour. And a certain man lame from his mother's womb was carried, whom they laid daily at the gate of the temple which is called Beautiful, to ask alms from those who entered the temple; who, seeing Peter and John about to go into the temple, asked for alms. And fixing his eyes on him, with John, Peter said, "Look at us." So he gave them his attention, expecting to receive something from them. Then Peter said, "Silver and gold I do not have, but what I do have I give you: In the name of Jesus Christ of Nazareth, rise up and walk." And he took him by the right hand and lifted him up, and immediately his feet and ankle bones received strength. So he, leaping up, stood and walked and entered the temple with them—walking, leaping, and praising God. And all the people saw him walking and praising God. Then they knew that it was he who sat begging alms at the Beautiful Gate of the temple; and they were filled with wonder and amazement at what had happened to him. Now as the lame man who was healed held on to Peter and John, all the people ran together to them in the porch which is called Solomon's, greatly amazed. So when Peter saw it, he responded to the people: "Men of Israel, why do you marvel at this? Or why look so intently at us, as though by our own power or godliness we had made this man walk? The God of Abraham, Isaac, and Jacob, the God of our fathers, glorified His Servant Jesus, whom you delivered up and denied in the presence of Pilate, when he was determined to let Him go. But you denied the Holy One and the Just, and asked for a murderer to be granted to you, and killed the Prince of life, whom God raised from the dead, of which we are witnesses. And His name, through faith in His name, has made this man strong, whom you see and know. Yes, the faith which comes through Him has given him this perfect soundness in the presence of you all.

~ *PRAYER* ~

Father, I thank You that I don't have to rely on my own power or godliness to receive my healing. It is not an issue of mind over matter. It is an issue of Your power flowing through me. It is an issue of faith that comes through Jesus that gives me perfect soundness. I acknowledge before You, Father, that it is by faith in Jesus alone that makes me completely whole.

———— DECLARATION OF FAITH ————

In every circumstance, no matter what my situation (what I have or do not have), I can use the name of Jesus to meet any of my needs.

All of the miracle-working power that flows through me is not my own. It is the power of God working in and through me doing those things that bring joy to His heart.

In and through the name of Jesus, I remain perfectly healthy and strong. And through His name, I have the ability to bring His healing power to all who will receive it.

(John 14:10-14; Philippians 2:10-13; 4:19; 1 John 5:14,15; Colossians 1:27-29; Ephesians 3:20; 6:10; 1 Peter 2:24; Mark 11:22-25; 16:17,18; Luke 9:1,2; Matthew 9:22)

ACTS 4:7-22

When they had set them in the midst, they asked, "By what power or by what name have you done this?" Then Peter, filled with the Holy Spirit, said to them, "Rulers of the people and elders of Israel: If we this day are judged for a good deed done to a helpless man, by what means he has been made well, let it be known to you all, and to all the people of Israel, that by the name of Jesus Christ of Nazareth, whom you crucified, whom God raised from the dead, by Him this man stands here before you whole. This is the 'stone which was rejected by you builders, which has become the chief cornerstone.' Nor is there salvation in any other, for there is no other name under heaven given among men by which we must be saved." Now when they saw the boldness of Peter and John, and perceived that they were uneducated and untrained men, they marveled. And they realized that they had been with Jesus. And seeing the man who had been healed standing with them, they could say nothing against it. But when they had commanded them to go aside out of the council, they conferred among themselves, saying, "What shall we do to these men? For, indeed, that a notable miracle has been done through them is evident to all who dwell in Jerusalem, and we cannot deny it. But so that it spreads no further among the people, let us severely threaten them, that from now on they speak to no man in this name." So they called them and commanded them not to speak at all nor teach in the name of Jesus. But Peter and John answered and said to them, "Whether it is right in the sight of God to listen to you more than to God, you judge. For we cannot but speak the things which we have seen and heard." So when they had further threatened them, they let them go, finding no way of punishing them, because of the people, since they all glorified God for what had been done. For the man was over forty years old on whom this miracle of healing had been performed.

~ PRAYER ~

Father, I have no shame to declare to the entire world that in the name of Jesus of Nazareth, I am saved, delivered, and healed. He is the stone that the builders rejected, but He has become the chief cornerstone of my life. I say without reservation, Father, that He is my Lord and my healer. He is my God and in Him do I trust. I will preach in His name, I will pray in His name, and I will receive my healing through His name. In Him I live and move and have my being. I shout glory to His name both now and forevermore!

──── DECLARATION OF FAITH ────

Let it be known and understood by all that it is in and through the name of Jesus that I stand whole, and through Him alone am I able to bring wholeness to others.

I have been granted the power of attorney to use the name of Jesus to meet every need.

Jesus, my Lord who was crucified and whom God raised from the dead, is the power by and through which I live. He is the chief corner-stone on which all that I am and all that I do is built. There is no enduring salvation of any kind apart from Him, for there is no other name under heaven, given among men, by which we can be saved. In and through Him, I have boldness to do what I am called to do, and furthermore, I have unfettered eloquence to answer any charge that is laid against me.

I cannot help but speak of this great salvation that I enjoy in Jesus. When governments and authorities tell me that I am not to converse in any way, or teach at all in or about the name of Jesus, I must rebel against them, for it is better in the eyes of God to obey Him and His commission rather than the foolish, anti-God rules of men.

(Mark 16:15-20; John 14:13,14; 15:7; 16:13,23,24; Galatians 2:20; Matthew 7:24; 28:18-20; Psalm 118:22; Romans 10:8-13; Acts 4:23-31; 5:28,29; 1 John 1:1-3)

Acts 4:23-31

And being let go, they went to their own companions and reported all that the chief priests and elders had said to them. So when they heard that, they raised their voice to God with one accord and said: "Lord, You are God, who made heaven and earth and the sea, and all that is in them, who by the mouth of Your servant David have said: 'Why did the nations rage, and the people plot vain things? The kings of the earth took their stand, and the rulers were gathered together against the LORD and against His Christ.' For truly against Your holy Servant Jesus, whom You anointed, both Herod and Pontius Pilate, with the Gentiles and the people of Israel, were gathered together to do whatever Your hand and Your purpose determined before to be done. Now, Lord, look on their threats, and grant to Your servants that with all boldness they may speak Your word, by stretching out Your hand to heal, and that signs and wonders may be done through the name of Your holy Servant Jesus." And when they had prayed, the place where they were assembled together was shaken; and they were all filled with the Holy Spirit, and they spoke the word of God with boldness.

~ PRAYER ~

Father, You are God, the Creator of every living being. You formed the worlds and by Your Word You hold all things together. I will not fear the wrath of evil men or the onslaughts of the unseen enemy. I have Your Word that no evil shall befall me and no plague can come near me. When the rulers and principalities gather together against me, I am laughing right along with You. How foolish it is to come against God and His chosen one.

Father, You see the attacks of the enemy and You know what I face. Now hold them in derision. Speak to them in Your wrath and distress them in Your deep displeasure. Place the fear and dread of me upon their hearts as I declare the authority of Your Word. Stretch out Your hand to heal, that signs and wonders may be done, in Jesus' name.

──── *DECLARATION OF FAITH* ────

When evil men (leaders in league with the devil) rise up and plot against me, I have the Word as my defense. There is an army of men, women, and angels ready to take their stand at my side. Together, we raise our voices in one accord to our God and Father, the sovereign Lord of the universe, who made the heavens, the earth, the sea, and all that is in them, including those who plot against me.

When I speak the Word to the problem, all of hell breaks loose. It is written (in Psalm 2) that when the heathen rage against me and plot my destruction, and the kings of the earth (spiritual ruling powers of darkness) assemble themselves against the Lord and His anointed (me), He who sits in heaven laughs. God himself observes their threats and takes His stand with me. He is on my side! Therefore, I declare His Word fearlessly, in the name of Jesus, and He stretches out His hand to perform signs, wonders, and miracles on my behalf!

(Romans 8:31,37; Mark 11:22-25; 16:15-20; 2 Corinthians 10:3-6; Acts 2:43; 5:12)

ACTS 5:14-16

And believers were increasingly added to the Lord, multitudes of both men and women, so that they brought the sick out into the streets and laid them on beds and couches, that at least the shadow of Peter passing by might fall on some of them. Also a multitude gathered from the surrounding cities to Jerusalem, bringing sick people and those who were tormented by unclean spirits, and they were all healed.

~ PRAYER ~

Father, Your ministry marches on. Add to our number daily those who will be saved. Heal the sick, raise the dead, and bring prosperity to Your church. Satan, I command your forces to leave my area of influence. Sickness and disease, you must flee. Health and prosperity, you must enter, in Jesus' name.

──── DECLARATION OF FAITH ────

The Holy Spirit performs many signs, wonders, and miracles by my hands and through the words that I speak (in accordance with the Scriptures).

I know the power of the corporate anointing; therefore, I regularly meet together with my other brothers and sisters in Christ.

Much respect is given to me by those outside of the kingdom because of the presence and power of the Holy Spirit who is within me.

I am an instrument of the Lord and I am used mightily to bring a great harvest of souls into the family of God.

People in the world regularly come to me to pray for them, for they know that the Lord hears my prayers and will grant them deliverance through me.

In Jesus, I have a reputation as a master of the forces of darkness. I am an ambassador of the Lord with the power to deliver and heal.

(Proverbs 11:30; 18:20,21; Mark 11:22-25; 16:15-20; Jeremiah 1:12; Isaiah 55:11; Hebrews 10:25; Proverbs 3:3,4; Acts 4:21; 19:11,12; Luke 10:19; 2 Corinthians 5:18-20)

ACTS 8:6-8

The multitudes with one accord heeded the things spoken by Philip, hearing and seeing the miracles which he did. For unclean spirits, crying with a loud voice, came out of many who were possessed; and many who were paralyzed and lame were healed. And there was great joy in that city.

~ PRAYER ~

Father, let's bring joy to my city. Stretch out Your hand through me to heal the sick. May those who are paralyzed walk. May those who are lame be made completely whole. Use me mightily, Father, as I advance Your kingdom with signs and wonders following.

—— DECLARATION OF FAITH ——

There are many people who will listen and heed the message that I give.

God is working in and through me in this endeavor, and signs and wonders are regularly manifested in my ministry. Even the crippled ones, bound to wheelchairs, have their strength restored and walk as well as any other.

All evil spirits must obey me and leave whenever I command them to.

There is continuous rejoicing in my city over the wonderful things that God is doing for us.

(Luke 10:19; Mark 16:15-20; Isaiah 61:1-3; John 14:12)

ACTS 9:33-35

There he found a certain man named Aeneas, who had been bedridden eight years and was paralyzed. And Peter said to him, "Aeneas, Jesus the Christ heals you. Arise and make your bed." Then he arose immediately. So all who dwelt at Lydda and Sharon saw him and turned to the Lord.

~ PRAYER ~

Father, I know that Jesus heals me. I speak to every nerve in my body and command them to be made whole. I know that paralysis is not beyond Your power. Therefore, heal paralysis, in Jesus' name. Bring forth a testimony that others may see and turn to You.

———— *DECLARATION OF FAITH* ————

Paralysis is no match for the name of Jesus. As Christ's ambassa-dor, with the power of attorney to use His name, I am well able to provide healing for the paralytic.

(Philippians 2:10; 2 Corinthians 5:18-20; John 14:13,14; Mark 16:17,18; Acts 3:1-10)

ACTS 10:34-38

Then Peter opened his mouth and said: "In truth I perceive that God shows no partiality. But in every nation whoever fears Him and works righteousness is accepted by Him. The word which God sent to the children of Israel, preaching peace through Jesus Christ—He is Lord of all—that word you know, which was proclaimed throughout all Judea, and began from Galilee after the baptism which John preached: how God anointed Jesus of Nazareth with the Holy Spirit and with power, who went about doing good and healing all who were oppressed by the devil, for God was with Him."

~ *PRAYER* ~

Father, thank You for accepting me and making me Your own. You do not show partiality. Your power is just as available to me as it is to any other. Everyone who trusts You and works righteousness You make Your very own. I am now in Jesus and His anointing is within me. I know that You are always with me. You never leave me nor forsake me.

Train me, Father, that I may go about doing good and healing all who are oppressed of the devil.

DECLARATION OF FAITH

God is not a respecter of persons. He does not see anyone as being above me, better than me, or more important than I am.

I am one among many equals in the body of Christ.

I am in Christ and it is my commission to continue His work in the earth. I have been anointed and consecrated by the Father with strength, ability, and power through the Holy Spirit and in Jesus' name. It is my duty to go about doing good and healing all who are oppressed of the devil, for God is with me.

(Romans 2:11; Ephesians 6:9; John 3:2; 14:10-12; 17:20-26;
2 Corinthians 5:18-20; Matthew 4:23; 28:18-20; Mark 16:15-20; Luke 9:1,2;
10:19; Acts 1:8; 1 John 2:20,27)

ACTS 14:8-10

In Lystra a certain man without strength in his feet was sitting, a cripple from his mother's womb, who had never walked. This man heard Paul speaking. Paul, observing him intently and seeing that he had faith to be healed, said with a loud voice, "Stand up straight on your feet!" And he leaped and walked.

~ *PRAYER* ~

Father, I know that faith comes by hearing Your Word again and again until I have a revealed understanding of it. Therefore, I will focus my attention on Your Word instead of things that waste my precious time. I'm not going to let the devil steal my healing with distractions and compromises. I know I can't receive my healing outside of faith. Faith does not come by listening to worldly music, watching ungodly movies and television shows, or engaging in unprofitable conversation. Faith comes by hearing and understanding Your Word. Strengthen me as I sow Your Word into my heart, Father. Heal me according to the precepts You have shown me.

──── *DECLARATION OF FAITH* ────

I am observant and discerning of those who have the faith to be healed. In accordance with the Word, I can speak into their bodies the healing that they need.

(Psalm 107:20; Mark 11:22-25; Acts 3:2-10; 1 John 5:14,15; 2 Corinthians 4:13)

ACTS 19:11,12

Now God worked unusual miracles by the hands of Paul, so that even handkerchiefs or aprons were brought from his body to the sick, and the diseases left them and the evil spirits went out of them.

~ PRAYER ~

Father, make Your anointing flow through me strongly. Bring forth unusual miracles by my hands. Make the anointing so strong that my very clothing contains Your healing power.

Father, increase my compassion for the hurting. Enlighten my perception of the devil's schemes that I may chase him out of my world, in Jesus' name.

───── DECLARATION OF FAITH ─────

God does unusual and extraordinary things by my hands. Because of His anointing within me, even when handkerchiefs, or the like, touch my hands, God's anointing is released into them. When these handkerchiefs are taken away and placed upon the sick, diseases leave them and evil spirits flee from them.

(Mark 16:15-20; Acts 5:15; Luke 9:1,2; 10:19; James 5:14-16)

ACTS 28:8,9

It happened that the father of Publius lay sick of a fever and dysentery. Paul went in to him and prayed, and he laid his hands on him and healed him. So when this was done, the rest of those on the island who had diseases also came and were healed.

~ PRAYER ~

Father, I thank You that I am healed of every sickness and disease. Fever cannot remain in my body. My body is healed and remains perfectly well. Your anointing, with its healing power, is within me at this very moment. It works both in me and through me. I not only have it for myself, but I can transfer it to others as well. Teach me discernment, Father. Give me the perception I need so that I may know who to lay hands on to dispense this great healing power that is within me.

––––––––– *DECLARATION OF FAITH* –––––––––

Jesus has given me complete authority over attacks of fever and dysentery. When I command them to leave, they must go, and when I call for the healing to come [in this context, through the laying on of my hands], it comes. People know this about me and come to me regularly to have me pray for them, for they know that I am called of God and have become one of His children. Respect, honor, and favor continually come to me because of my integrity and uncompromising character. In Jesus, I am always well provided for and have everything that I need.

(Luke 9:1,2; 10:17-19; John 14:13,14; Mark 11:22-25; James 5:14-16; Proverbs 3:3,4; Exodus 3:21,22; 11:3; 12:36; 1 Timothy 5:17; Philippians 4:19)

ACTS 28:24-27

Some were persuaded by the things which were spoken, and some disbelieved. So when they did not agree among themselves, they departed after Paul had said one word: "The Holy Spirit spoke rightly through Isaiah the prophet to our fathers, saying, 'Go to this people and say: "Hearing you will hear, and shall not understand; And seeing you will see, and not perceive; For the hearts of this people have grown dull. Their ears are hard of hearing, and their eyes they have closed, lest they should see with their eyes and hear with their ears, lest they should understand with their hearts and turn, so that I should heal them."'"

~ PRAYER ~

Father, I know that belief is a choice. It is not a matter of evidence or proof. It is a matter of choice. I understand that faith believes in spite of the physical evidence. Therefore, I make my choice and turn to You. I declare in harmony with Your Word that I am healed. There is no more discussion needed. I choose to believe You, Father. I have faith that You will make good on what You have said.

—— DECLARATION OF FAITH ——

I am not a person who turns a deaf ear to the truth. I do not walk by sight; I walk by faith. My heart is sharp and discerning. My spiritual eyes are wide open; I see and perceive the truth. I see with my eyes, hear with my ears, and understand with my heart. The Word says that I am healed. Therefore, I am healed.

(Isaiah 6:8-10; 53:3-5; 61:1-3; Matthew 8:16,17; Ephesians 1:17-23)

CHAPTER TWENTY-ONE

ROMANS

ROMANS 4:16-21

Therefore it is of faith that it might be according to grace, so that the promise might be sure to all the seed, not only to those who are of the law, but also to those who are of the faith of Abraham, who is the father of us all (as it is written, "I have made you a father of many nations") in the presence of Him whom he believed—God, who gives life to the dead and calls those things which do not exist as though they did; who, contrary to hope, in hope believed, so that he became the father of many nations, according to what was spoken, "So shall your descendants be." And not being weak in faith, he did not consider his own body, already dead (since he was about a hundred years old), and the deadness of Sarah's womb. He did not waver at the promise of God through unbelief, but was strengthened in faith, giving glory to God, and being fully convinced that what He had promised He was also able to perform.

~ PRAYER ~

Thank You, Father, for giving me surety in my prayers. I receive from You on the basis of faith alone. Your promise to me is made sure by grace (unmerited, underserved favor). All I need to do is believe what You have said and act on that belief. You give life to the dead and call those things that be not as though they were. When I set myself in agreement with You, You cause Your Word to be fulfilled in me. I choose to believe, Father. I will not be weak in faith by considering what my body feels like or what the report of the doctors says. I believe You. I will not waver at Your promise. I stand strong in faith, giving You the glory that You deserve. I am fully convinced that what You have promised You are able to perform. Your Word is truth, not my circumstances. By Jesus' stripes I am healed.

——— DECLARATION OF FAITH ———

My inheritance of God's promise is the outcome of my faith. By believing in the promise and speaking of it as if it were mine, God has an avenue to give it to me as an act of grace (unmerited, unde-served favor). This overcomes the obstacles that imprison God's giving heart and is the surety that guarantees that I will receive His promise in my life.

I walk in the faith of Abraham (the father of my faith). Abraham understood the faith of God, in whom he believed—the very One who brings life out of death by calling those things that be not as though they are. When God declared, "I have made you a father of many nations," Abraham's hope was not shaken. He did not say, "No, God, You're a liar, because I obviously don't have any children." To the contrary, he did not weaken in faith by looking at his body, which was as good as dead, but against all hope and circumstance, he had the assurance of his faith, believing in the promise and speaking of it as if it were already fulfilled.

When God said, "Look to the stars, Abraham. So shall your descendents be," He gave Abraham a vision of his destiny. Abraham, the father of my faith, with his finger pointing to the heavens, declared in triumphal harmony with God, "So shall my descendents be!" Like God, regardless of his natural circumstances, he called those things that be not as though they were.

This is the example set before me. I believe and declare God's Word to be true in my life. Therefore, in faith, I call those things which be not [in my present condition or circumstance] as if I already have them. I will allow no unbelief or mistrust to make me waver, but shall grow strong, empowered by faith, giving praise and glory to God.

I believe that God is trustworthy and I am fully convinced that He is able to keep His Word and do what He has promised.

I am the righteousness of God in Christ Jesus. This righteousness is granted to me because I believe in and put my total reliance upon God, who raised Jesus my Lord from the dead. It was Jesus who took my place, was betrayed and put to death because of my sin, but was raised again once my justification was secured, and it is by Jesus alone that my healing is absolutely guaranteed.

(2 Corinthians 4:13; 5:7,21; Hebrews 11:1,6,11,14; Romans 3:24; 8:11; 9:26; Galatians 3:22; Genesis 17:17; Mark 11:22-25; Isaiah 53:4,5; 1 Corinthians 15:17)

ROMANS 8:10,11

If Christ is in you, the body is dead because of sin, but the Spirit is life because of righteousness. But if the Spirit of Him who raised Jesus from the dead dwells in you, He who raised Christ from the dead will also give life to your mortal bodies through His Spirit who dwells in you.

~ PRAYER ~

Father, You have made me one with my Lord Jesus. The Anointed One and His anointing dwell within me. This body may be as good as dead because of sin, but my spirit is charged with eternal life because of Jesus' righteousness. The very power that raised Jesus from the dead gives life to this mortal body through His Spirit who dwells within me.

──── DECLARATION OF FAITH ────

I am not controlled by the flesh, or the natural desires of my old nature, but by my recreated spirit where the very Spirit of God dwells.

Jesus himself dwells within me.

The old sinful nature that was once me is dead because of sin, but my recreated spirit is fully alive because of righteousness.

The Spirit of the One who raised Jesus from the dead dwells within me, and through that same resurrection power, He gives life (health and vitality) to this mortal body in which I dwell.

I no longer have to live by what is natural (the laws of nature established in my flesh), for those ways are the ways of death (producing the things of death). Through my spirit (led by the Holy Spirit), I kill off all of those practices that are one with death [and produce the things of death], and I live my life in the way that produces the things of life in me.

(Galatians 2:20,21; 6:8; 1 Corinthians 5:17,21; Ephesians 1:17-23; 4:22)

ROMANS 10:8-11

But what does it say? "The word is near you, in your mouth and in your heart" (that is, the word of faith which we preach): that if you confess with your mouth the Lord Jesus and believe in your heart that God has raised Him from the dead, you will be saved. For with the heart one believes unto righteousness, and with the mouth confession is made unto salvation. For the Scripture says, "Whoever believes on Him will not be put to shame."

~ *PRAYER* ~

Father, I choose to believe. I know that Your Word will accomplish the task for which You sent it. Therefore, I speak it with my mouth and believe it with my heart. I am healed, in Jesus' name.

——— *DECLARATION OF FAITH* ———

My righteousness is founded on faith.

It is now totally unnecessary for me to try to bombard the gates of heaven in order to be saved or receive from God. I am always welcome at my Father's throne.

It is also ludicrous for me to expect Jesus to suffer over and over again every time I mess up. His sacrifice has made me righteous once and for all.

The way of justification, salvation, healing, and blessing is not put at a distance from me. As it is written, the Word is very near to me—it is on my lips and in my heart. I make my confession by the Word of faith. If I confess with my mouth the Lordship of Jesus and believe in my heart that God has raised Him from the dead, I shall be saved and delivered from every circumstance beginning with salvation from spiritual death; for it is with my heart that I believe unto justification and righteousness, and it is with my mouth that I confess, bringing forth my salvation and deliverance. As it is written, "Anyone who puts their faith in Him shall never be put to shame." Through this process, my Lord richly blesses me with all things, for everyone who calls on His name shall be saved.

(Hebrews 4:15,16; 10:10,14; 11:1,6; Romans 1:17; 3:21,22; 4:11; 5:1,2; 8:32; 9:30; Deuteronomy 30:12-14; Luke 12:8; Mark 11:22-25; 2 Corinthians 4:13; 5:7; Jeremiah 1:12; Matthew 21:19-22; Ephesians 1:7,17-23; Joel 2:32; Acts 2:21,38,39; 2 Peter 1:3)

ROMANS 15:13

Now may the God of hope fill you with all joy and peace in believing, that you may abound in hope by the power of the Holy Spirit.

~ *PRAYER* ~

Father, Your joy is my strength. I have confidence in Your Word. I abound in hope by the power of the Holy Spirit!

─────── *DECLARATION OF FAITH* ───────

My heavenly Father, the God of all hope, fills me with all joy and peace as I believe in Him. I overflow with hope through the Holy Spirit who is within me.

In Him, I am full of goodness, complete in knowledge, and well able to teach others the things that I know.

(Romans 14:17; Ephesians 2:14; Philippians 4:7; 1 Timothy 1:1; 1 John 2:20; 2 Peter 1:12; 1 Corinthians 1:5,30)

CHAPTER TWENTY-TWO

1 CORINTHIANS

1 CORINTHIANS 11:27-31

Therefore whoever eats this bread or drinks this cup of the Lord in an unworthy manner will be guilty of the body and blood of the Lord. But let a man examine himself, and so let him eat of the bread and drink of the cup. For he who eats and drinks in an unworthy manner eats and drinks judgment to himself, not discerning the Lord's body. For this reason many are weak and sick among you, and many sleep. For if we would judge ourselves, we would not be judged.

~ PRAYER ~

Father, I know that the Lord's Supper represents the body of Jesus that was broken for me and the blood of the new covenant that was shed for me. Whenever I eat the bread and drink the cup, I discern the Lord's death until He comes. Far be it from me, Father, to partake of this observance in an unworthy manner. I love my Lord and I am ever-grateful for what He did for me. When I partake of this bread and this cup, it is with reverence, awe, and utter appreciation.

──── *DECLARATION OF FAITH* ────

I will not partake of the Lord's Supper in an unworthy manner
and thereby be guilty of the body and blood of the Lord. I examine
myself and discern the Lord's body. I will not eat and drink judgment to
myself and end up getting sick or even dying.

(Matthew 26:26,27; Mark 14:22-24; Luke 22:14-21)

1 CORINTHIANS 12:7-11

But the manifestation of the Spirit is given to each one for the profit
of all: for to one is given the word of wisdom through the Spirit, to
another the word of knowledge through the same Spirit, to another
faith by the same Spirit, to another gifts of healings by the same Spirit,
to another the working of miracles, to another prophecy, to another
discerning of spirits, to another different kinds of tongues, to another
the interpretation of tongues. But one and the same Spirit works all
these things, distributing to each one individually as He wills.

~ PRAYER ~

Father, I thank You that the Holy Spirit dwells within me and His
power works through me as He wills. In Him there is righteousness,
peace, joy, and all manner of precious gifts. No matter what I need,
You richly provide—all praise be to Your holy name.

———— DECLARATION OF FAITH ————

I fully understand that there are many different gifts that the Spirit gives and that any one of them can work in my life at any given moment. I also know that no spiritual gift operates in my life but that which is given to me for the common good and edification of all.

Though I may operate in any spiritual gift, I have no monopoly on them in the assembly (in church). I may speak a word of wisdom, a word of knowledge, operate in supernatural faith, perform healings, display miraculous powers, prophesy, discern spirits that are present [distinguish between them or receive some revelation of them], prophesy in tongues, or give the interpretation of prophetic tongues, but only as the Spirit leads.

(1 Corinthians 14:1-5; 15:28; Mark 16:17,18; Acts 1:8; Romans 12:6)

CHAPTER TWENTY-THREE

2 CORINTHIANS

2 CORINTHIANS 12:7-10

And lest I should be exalted above measure by the abundance of the revelations, a thorn in the flesh was given to me, a messenger of Satan to buffet me, lest I be exalted above measure. Concerning this thing I pleaded with the Lord three times that it might depart from me. And He said to me, "My grace is sufficient for you, for My strength is made perfect in weakness." Therefore most gladly I will rather boast in my infirmities, that the power of Christ may rest upon me. Therefore I take pleasure in infirmities, in reproaches, in needs, in persecutions, in distresses, for Christ's sake. For when I am weak, then I am strong.

~ PRAYER ~

Father, in You I have no fear of Satan's emissaries. Your grace is sufficient for me and Your strength is made perfect in my weaknesses. I don't have to worry about how well I can do things or if I have enough power to overcome. You are my power, Lord. In You, I have already overcome. I'm not going to worry about the struggles that I endure.

Whenever I am weak, I have Your strength to see me through. Therefore, no matter what I face, the victory is mine.

─────── *DECLARATION OF FAITH* ───────

God's grace (divine enabling) is all that I need to stand in perpetual victory in this life; for His strength in me is made perfect in my weakness. Therefore, even when I am weak, the strength and power of Christ rests on me. This is why I delight in my weaknesses as a man/woman and why hardships, persecutions, and difficulties can't cause me to become distressed; for when I recognize my own weakness, I know to rely on His strength. And in His strength, I am not a victim, but a victor—a champion made to display God's own glory to the world!

(Romans 5:1,2; 8:31,37; 1 Peter 4:14; Colossians 1:27-29; 1 Corinthians 13:4)

CHAPTER TWENTY-FOUR

GALATIANS

GALATIANS 3:13,14

Christ has redeemed us from the curse of the law, having become a curse for us (for it is written, "Cursed is everyone who hangs on a tree"), that the blessing of Abraham might come upon the Gentiles in Christ Jesus, that we might receive the promise of the Spirit through faith.

~ PRAYER ~

Father, I thank You that I am redeemed from the curse of the law. All of those curses of sickness, disease, and disaster no longer apply to me because I am in Christ Jesus and He has set me free! The blessing of Abraham is upon me and I have received the promise of the Spirit through faith!

── DECLARATION OF FAITH ──

I consider Abraham a chief role model for my faith. As it is written, "He believed God and it was credited to him as righteousness."

In this respect, as a believer I am a child of Abraham. The Scripture foresaw that God would justify me through faith, and He announced the gospel to Abraham all those many years ago, saying, "All nations will be blessed through you." Therefore, as a man/woman of faith, I am blessed in the same ways that Abraham was, for he is the father of my faith.

I will not put myself back under the Law, thereby putting myself under the curse, for it is written, "Cursed is anyone who does not continually (without fail) do everything written in the Book of the Law." Therefore, it is abundantly clear that I cannot be justified by the Law because I, along with everyone else in this world, have failed to keep it at one time or another.

As a seal to this truth, it is also written, "The righteous shall live by faith," and, "The man who lives by the Law must never fail in it." Therefore, with the Law and faith being clearly contrary to each other, I will not allow myself to rely on my own deeds of righteousness to justify me before God.

Jesus redeemed me from the curse of the Law, being made a curse for me, for it is written, "Cursed is the one who is hung on a tree."

He redeemed me so that, through Him, I could receive the same blessings that were showered upon Abraham, and so that through faith I could receive the promise of the Spirit.

Just as no one can add to or set aside a human covenant once it has been established (witnessed and notarized), so it is in this case. The promises were spoken to Abraham and his Seed. It does not say, "To his seeds," meaning many people, but, "To his Seed," meaning one person, who is Jesus. And since He became my substitute and I am now one *with Him, I am a recipient of those promises. Because of what Jesus did for me, all of God's promises are now mine through Him. Praise God, every promise of healing is now mine, in Jesus name!*

(Genesis 12:1-3,16; 13:2,6; 15:1,6,15; 17:1,2,6-9; 18:27; 20:7; 24:35; 26:3,12-14; Hebrews 11:1,6; Romans 3:21-26; 4:1-4; 8:1-4; 11:6; Deuteronomy 21:23; 27:26; 28:15-68; Leviticus 18:5; Ephesians 1:3,4,7,11,13,14; 2:13-15; 6:10; John 17:6-26; 2 Corinthians 1:20)

CHAPTER TWENTY-FIVE

EPHESIANS

＋

EPHESIANS 1:3

Blessed be the God and Father of our Lord Jesus Christ, who has blessed us with every spiritual blessing in the heavenly places in Christ.

~ *PRAYER* ~

Father, I bless You who have blessed me with every spiritual blessing in the heavenly places in Christ. All of Your blessings are contained in the anointing that is within me. All of my needs have already been met. Teach me to operate in Your precepts, Father, so that I may enjoy every one!

——— *DECLARATION OF FAITH* ———

I give all praise, honor, and glory to my God, the Father of my Lord Jesus, for He has blessed me with every spiritual blessing in Christ.

(2 Corinthians 1:20; Galatians 3:6-16; 2 Peter 1:3)

EPHESIANS 1:15-23

Therefore I also, after I heard of your faith in the Lord Jesus and your love for all the saints, do not cease to give thanks for you, making mention of you in my prayers: that the God of our Lord Jesus Christ, the Father of glory, may give to you the spirit of wisdom and revelation in the knowledge of Him, the eyes of your understanding being enlightened; that you may know what is the hope of His calling, what are the riches of the glory of His inheritance in the saints, and what is the exceeding greatness of His power toward us who believe, according to the working of His mighty power which He worked in Christ when He raised Him from the dead and seated Him at His right hand in the heavenly places, far above all principality and power and might and dominion, and every name that is named, not only in this age but also in that which is to come. And He put all things under His feet, and gave Him to be head over all things to the church, which is His body, the fullness of Him who fills all in all.

~ PRAYER ~

Father, I thank You that Jesus has become my wisdom, my righteousness, my sanctification, and my redemption. I thank You for giving me wisdom and revelation in the knowledge of You; that the eyes of my understanding are enlightened and I know the hope of my calling and what are the riches of the glory of Your inheritance that has been granted to me, and what is the exceeding greatness of Your power toward me. I know now that the very power that flows within me is the power that was at work in Christ when You raised Him from the dead and seated Him at Your own right hand, far above any principality, power, might, or dominion; far above any name that can be named. I have that power now and I have it for all of eternity. All things have been placed under Christ's feet. He is the head and I am the body—the fullness of Him who fills me in every way.

――――― *DECLARATION OF FAITH* ―――――

My heavenly Father has given me a spirit of wisdom and revelation, of insight into mysteries and secrets, in the deep and intimate knowledge of Himself. My spirit has been enlightened with a flood of understanding so that I can know and comprehend the hope of my calling and the immense riches of this glorious inheritance that has become my own.

I now have a complete understanding of the exceeding greatness of His power toward me. The power that is now residing and working within me is the very power that God wrought in Christ when He raised Him from the dead and seated Him at His own right hand, far above every principality, every power, every ruler of darkness, all dominion, and every name or title that can be given. And this power is not only working in and through me now, but it will continue to work in and through me in the age to come. As God has placed all things under Jesus' feet and appointed Him to be the head of the body (the church), I have now, as a part of His body, become the fullness of Jesus in this earth as He fills me in every way. All things are placed under my feet, and every power and dominion must obey me as I apply the power of attorney that Jesus has given me to use His name.

(Daniel 2:22,23; 1 Corinthians 1:30; 2:6-16; Matthew 13:11,15,16; 1 John 2:20,27; 5:20; Romans 8:17; 1 Peter 1:3-5; Colossians 1:9-18,26-29; Philippians 2:5-13; John 14:13,14; 17:20-26; Ephesians 2:6; Hebrews 2:5-14; Luke 10:19; Mark 16:15-20)

CHAPTER TWENTY-SIX

PHILIPPIANS

PHILIPPIANS 2:25-27

I considered it necessary to send to you Epaphroditus, my brother, fellow worker, and fellow soldier, but your messenger and the one who ministered to my need; since he was longing for you all, and was distressed because you had heard that he was sick. For indeed he was sick almost unto death; but God had mercy on him, and not only on him but on me also, lest I should have sorrow upon sorrow.

~ PRAYER ~

Father, I thank You that You have mercy on me. No matter what I face, I have Your grace. Sin cannot lord sickness over me. I am in Christ Jesus and He has set me free.

——— DECLARATION OF FAITH ———

Sickness cannot kill me. For me, there is no sickness that will lead to my death. God has mercy on me and will raise me from any attack the devil tries to use against me.

(Psalms 79:11; 107:18-20; Mark 5:21-43)

CHAPTER TWENTY-SEVEN

1 THESSALONIANS

1 THESSALONIANS 2:13,14

For this reason we also thank God without ceasing, because when you received the word of God which you heard from us, you welcomed it not as the word of men, but as it is in truth, the word of God, which also effectively works in you who believe. For you, brethren, became imitators of the churches of God which are in Judea in Christ Jesus. For you also suffered the same things from your own countrymen, just as they did from the Judeans.

~ PRAYER ~

Father, I know that my Bible is not the words of men. It is Your Word, Father. It is the very Word of the Almighty and it effectively works in me. All of the great and precious promises that You have given are working in me at this very moment. Through Your Word, I have peace, healing, prosperity, and good things of every kind.

——— DECLARATION OF FAITH ———

I have received the Word, not as the word of men, but as the Word of God. At this very moment it is at work within me to accomplish the purpose for which God sent it.

(Galatians 4:14; 6:1,2; Ephesians 4:1-3; 1 Corinthians 1:9; Mark 4:20; 1 Peter 1:23; Isaiah 55:11)

CHAPTER TWENTY-EIGHT

1 TIMOTHY

1 TIMOTHY 5:23

No longer drink only water, but use a little wine[1] for your stomach's sake and your frequent infirmities.

~ PRAYER ~

Father, You are so good. The fact that You want me well is so abundantly evident. All through Your Word You give me examples of Your true heart and how You want me to live in health and prosperity. You even offer natural remedies to keep me from suffering from sickness and infirmities. Thank You, Father. I truly appreciate all that You have done for me.

—— DECLARATION OF FAITH ——

I am not against taking medicine or other remedies that promote my health. I know that it is my Father's will that I be healthy; therefore, I will do whatever I can to stay that way.

(Matthew 8:2,3; James 5:14-16; Isaiah 53:4,5; 1 Peter 2:24; Psalm 103:1-5; Exodus 15:26; 23:25)

CHAPTER TWENTY-NINE

HEBREWS

HEBREWS 11:1,6

Now faith is the substance of things hoped for; the evidence of things not seen… But without faith it is impossible to please Him, for he who comes to God must believe that He is, and that He is a rewarder of those who diligently seek Him.

~ PRAYER ~

Father, over and over again I have seen in Your Word that I am to live above my circumstances. Instill in me a revelation that I live in more than one world. This natural world does not supply my needs. All that I enjoy comes from the Spirit first; therefore, I know that the natural world is not the final authority. My final authority, Father, is Your Word. What You have promised is what I live by. I walk by faith and not by sight. No matter what my situation looks like, I will overcome and emerge victorious, in Jesus' name.

———— *DECLARATION OF FAITH* ————

My faith is the very substance of the things that I hope for. It is the certainty that what I do not see will soon be manifested in my life.

I have a thorough understanding of the process of faith. I understand that through faith, God created the universe with His Word. All that I see now was made out of what cannot be seen by the physical eye.

God has called me to live by the same process. When I believe and speak in perfect alignment with the will of God, the things that I say are manifested.

I know that without faith it is impossible for me to please God. In order for me to draw near to Him, I must first believe that He exists, and then that He will reward me as I diligently seek Him. I believe both. I have assurance in my heart that His Word rings true in my life. Therefore, I fix all of my will on pleasing Him in every way. To do this, I must make demands on the power that He has given me and call those things that be not as though they were.

(Mark 11:22-25; James 1:22-25; 2:17-26; 5:14-16; John 6:63; Matthew 21:19-22)

HEBREWS 12:12,13

Therefore strengthen the hands which hang down, and the feeble knees, and make straight paths for your feet, so that what is lame may not be dislocated, but rather be healed.

~ *PRAYER* ~

Father, I see by this Scripture that You are the God of order. Sickness, feebleness, lameness, and all infirmity bring confusion and disorder. They hinder the advancement of Your kingdom. Therefore, I know that they are not from You.

I will keep my eyes focused on the path You have set before me, Father. Your Word is the lamp unto my feet and the light unto my path. I send it forth to heal all confusion and disorder in my life.

—— DECLARATION OF FAITH ——

My heavenly Father only disciplines and reprimands me for my own good. He doesn't use sickness, disease, and disaster against me, but as a good Father, He disciplines me in order to protect me from such things. All of His discipline is designed with my holiness and well being in mind.[1] And though at times the training is very hard and taxing, it will later produce in me an abundant harvest of righteousness and peace.

Therefore, I am not dispirited or discouraged, but I am strengthened and encouraged. Through the Lord's discipline, I make level all the paths for my feet so that the way is made for me to walk in perfect health and happiness.

(Psalm 103:1-5,13; Leviticus 11:44; Matthew 6:10; James 3:17,18; Isaiah 35:1-10)

CHAPTER THIRTY

JAMES

JAMES 2:14-26

What does it profit, my brethren, if someone says he has faith but does not have works? Can faith save him? If a brother or sister is naked and destitute of daily food, and one of you says to them, "Depart in peace, be warmed and filled," but you do not give them the things which are needed for the body, what does it profit? Thus also faith by itself, if it does not have works, is dead. But someone will say, "You have faith, and I have works." Show me your faith without your works, and I will show you my faith by my works. You believe that there is one God. You do well. Even the demons believe—and tremble! But do you want to know, O foolish man, that faith without works is dead? Was not Abraham our father justified by works when he offered Isaac his son on the altar? Do you see that faith was working together with his works, and by works faith was made perfect? And the Scripture was fulfilled which says, "Abraham believed God, and it was accounted to him for righteousness." And he was called the friend of God. You see then that a man is justified by works, and not by faith only. Likewise, was not Rahab the harlot also justified by works when she received the messengers and sent them out another way? For as the body without the spirit is dead, so faith without works is dead also.

~ PRAYER ~

Father, I am not so foolish as to say I have faith and not have the works to back it. I believe in what You have said and I act on it. I show that my faith is genuine by the things that I do.

——— DECLARATION OF FAITH ———

I do more than just pray for the needs of the poor—I see to their needs as well. I give of my substance with a willing and cheerful heart, seeing to it that their needs are met through my deeds and not just my words.

In the same way, I maintain a working faith. I do not just give mental assent to the truth of the Word, but I act upon it, bearing an abundance of righteous fruit in my life. My faith has value only in the fruit that it produces.

(2 Corinthians 4:13; 5:7,21; 8:2-5; 9:5-11; 1 John 3:16-18; James 1:22-25; Matthew 7:17-19; John 1:12; 15:5-8,16; 16:23,24; 2 Chronicles 20:7; Colossians 2:6-8)

JAMES 5:13-16

Is anyone among you suffering? Let him pray. Is anyone cheerful? Let him sing psalms. Is anyone among you sick? Let him call for the elders of the church, and let them pray over him, anointing him with oil in the name of the Lord. And the prayer of faith will save the sick, and the Lord will raise him up. And if he has committed sins, he will be forgiven. Confess your trespasses to one another, and pray for one another, that you may be healed. The effective, fervent prayer of a righteous man avails much.

~ *PRAYER* ~

Father, I know that sickness and disease sadden Your heart. You want Your kids to live prosperous and healthy lives. In all that I do, Father, I want to please You and bring You joy. Therefore, I will not allow sickness to remain in my body. I will pray in faith and receive my healing. I will call for the elders of the church to anoint me with oil in the name of Jesus. My prayers shall remain white hot with faith and effectual in their working. I am not one to give up or give in, Father. I will do whatever it takes to stay prosperous and healthy all the days of my life.

—— DECLARATION OF FAITH ——

I will not face any trouble, adversity, or misfortune without prayer.

I continually sing songs of praise, rejoicing in what God has done in my life.

I have no need to fret over sickness, for even if it were to overwhelm me, I could call for the elders of the church and have them pray over me, anointing me with oil in the name of the Lord. I know that the prayer of faith will save the sick and the Lord shall raise them up. Therefore, if my faith is lacking, I will simply go where faith is strong in order to build myself back up, for it is abundantly clear that God wants me well.

If I have stumbled in any way, I do not need to fret over it—I can rest in full confidence that the Lord loves me and forgives all of my shortcomings.

I also know that sin is a hindrance to my healing. Therefore, if there is any sin in my life, I repent of it. I confess my sins to trusted brothers and sisters in Christ, gaining strength and praying in agreement with them so that I receive my healing.

(Ephesians 5:19; 6:18; 1 Thessalonians 5:16-18; Psalms 50:14; 89:20-23; 103:1-5; Isaiah 53:4,5; 1 Peter 2:24; Matthew 9:22,29; 18:19,20; Mark 11:22-26; 16:18; Hebrews 12:1-3; Galatians 6:1,2)

CHAPTER THIRTY-ONE

1 PETER

＋

1 PETER 2:21-25

For to this you were called, because Christ also suffered for us, leaving us an example, that you should follow His steps: "Who committed no sin, Nor was deceit found in His mouth"; who, when He was reviled, did not revile in return; when He suffered, He did not threaten, but committed Himself to Him who judges righteously; who Himself bore our sins in His own body on the tree, that we, having died to sins, might live for righteousness—by whose stripes you were healed. For you were like sheep going astray, but have now returned to the Shepherd and Overseer of your souls.

~ PRAYER ~

Father, I am ever so grateful for all that You have done for me. Teach me the way of righteousness, Lord. I know that I have died to sin and now live for righteousness. I know that by Jesus' stripes I am made whole. I have returned to You, Father, the Shepherd and

Overseer of my soul. I commit myself to live by Your precepts all the days of my life.

———— *DECLARATION OF FAITH* ————

It is commendable before God when I patiently persevere through unjust suffering.

To this I have been called: to follow in the footsteps of Jesus, who suffered for me, leaving me an example of how to endure it; for it is written: "He committed no sin, and no deceit was found in His mouth." When they hurled their insults at Him, He did not retaliate; and when He suffered, He made no threats. Instead, He entrusted Himself to Him who judges justly.

Knowing Jesus' reward, I too patiently endure unjust and unfair treatment, for I know that God is on my side. He is the One whom I am working for and the One who will reward and promote me.

Jesus bore my sins in His own body while on the cross so that I might die to sin and live unto righteousness. Through His torment and agony, I was healed (cured; made whole).

I was once like a runaway lamb, but now I have returned to the Shepherd and Overseer of my soul.

(Isaiah 53:4,5,9; Matthew 8:17; Hebrews 9:28; Ezekiel 34:23; James 1:2-4; Luke 6:32-34; Romans 8:31; 12:14-21; Colossians 3:17)

CHAPTER THIRTY-TWO

1 JOHN

1 JOHN 5:4

For whatever is born of God overcomes the world. And this is the victory that has overcome the world—our faith.

~ PRAYER ~

Father, I am Your son/daughter. I am born into Your family and I live by the family code. I overcome the world, the flesh, and the devil by living the very way that You live: by faith.

——— DECLARATION OF FAITH ———

I have been born of God and have overcome the world. My faith is my victory. All circumstance must yield to it. Through my faith, I overcome obstacles, setbacks, problems, and troubles of every kind.

I believe that Jesus is the Son of God, and in Him I have overcome the world.

(John 1:12,13; 14:15; 15:9-17; 16:33; Romans 12:9,10; Hebrews 10:24,25; 11:1-6; 1 John 2:13; Matthew 11:28-30; Psalm 119:160-165; 2 Corinthians 4:13; 5:7; Mark 11:22-25; Revelation 12:11)

CHAPTER THIRTY-THREE

3 JOHN

3 JOHN 2-4

Beloved, I pray that you may prosper in all things and be in health, just as your soul prospers. For I rejoiced greatly when brethren came and testified of the truth that is in you, just as you walk in the truth. I have no greater joy than to hear that my children walk in truth.

~ PRAYER ~

Father, in this final verse Your heart once again is revealed. You wish above all things that I prosper and remain in good health, even as my soul prospers. This is the truth and You have no greater joy than to see me walking in the truth. Thank You for my healing, Father. In Jesus' name, amen.

—— DECLARATION OF FAITH ——

I know the heart of my Father—that He is a good Father and wishes above all things that I prosper and remain healthy, even as my soul prospers.

It brings great joy to my heart when God's children are walking in the truth.

(Psalms 35:27; 103:1-5; 112:1-10; Deuteronomy 8:18; 28:1-14; Galatians 3:13,14; Genesis 12:1-3; 13:2; Isaiah 53:4,5; 2 Corinthians 9:5-11; 1 Peter 2:24; Colossians 2:19; 1 Thessalonians 3:12)

"Be of good cheer my brother/sister. Your faith has made you well. Go in shalom!"

CONCLUSION

Fear not! God's Word will not return void!

I can guarantee that the devil absolutely hates the fact that you have believed for your healing. Now he is going to do all that he can to try and get you to worry and start walking in fear. Some of the strategies he will use are:

Trying to get you to look at your circumstances, or other distractions, instead of the Word. (Mark 4:14-20.)

Putting faithless people in your path who try to get you to stop believing. (Mark 5:36.)

Trying to get you to listen to false teaching that acknowledges God but denies His power in the life of the believer. (2 Timothy 3:5.)

Trying to get you to think negative thoughts and speak negative words that are contrary to the Word of God. (James 3:2-5; Mark 11:22-24.)

Putting all kinds of fear and terror in your heart and mind because he knows that fear cancels faith and that without faith you cannot receive your healing. (Matthew 8:26; Luke 8:50.)

Trying to get you to walk in strife and unforgiveness—two of fear's faith-ending offspring. (Mark 11:25,26; 2 Timothy 2:23-26.)

Trying to put the ailment back on you when your guard is down. (Matthew 12:43-45.)

Trying to get you to think God doesn't want you well. (Matthew 8:1-3.)

Trying to get you to think that you are unworthy and have no right to be healed. (Galatians 3:1-5.)

Every time we win a battle, the devil and his forces regroup and seek an opportune time for a counterattack. (See Luke 4:13.) This is not a problem, however, because God has given you a whole arsenal of "fear not" promises. So whenever the devil tries to bring in his fear and doubt, attack him with the promises and declarations of faith on the pages following and you'll put him on the run every time.

JOSHUA 1:5-9

"No man shall be able to stand before you all the days of your life; as I was with Moses, so I will be with you. I will not leave you nor forsake you. Be strong and of good courage, for to this people you shall divide as an inheritance the land which I swore to their fathers to give them. Only be strong and very courageous, that you may observe to do according to all the law which Moses My servant commanded you; do not turn from it to the right hand or to the left, that you may prosper wherever you go. This Book of the Law shall not depart from your mouth, but you shall meditate in it day and night, that you may observe to do according to all that is written in it. For then you will make your way prosperous, and then you will have good success.

Have I not commanded you? Be strong and of good courage; do not be afraid, nor be dismayed, for the LORD your God is with you wherever you go."

──────── *DECLARATION OF FAITH* ────────

Through all the days of my life, not one of my enemies will be able to stand against me.

My Father is with me. Even more so, He has taken up residence inside of me. Therefore, I will be strong and courageous. I have complete confidence in His ability to give me the victory. I encounter danger and difficulties with firmness and without fear. I am bold, brave, and resolute. I fulfill my calling in a spirit of valor and determination that overcomes any obstacle that the enemy would put in my path.

I do not turn from God's Word. I make it the cornerstone of my life so that I may prosper in all that I do.

I speak the Word continually. I meditate upon it day and night so that I may do all that is written therein. By this, I make my way prosperous, have good success, and deal wisely in all of the affairs of my life.

I do not shrink back from God's Word. I am faithful, strong, vigorous, bold, and very courageous! Fear has no place in my life, for the Lord is with me wherever I go!

(Romans 8:31-37; Ephesians 3:16-19; Hebrew 6:12; Deuteronomy 31:6,7; Psalm 1:1-3; Isaiah 41:10)

ISAIAH 43:1-7

But now, thus says the LORD, who created you, O Jacob, and He who formed you, O Israel: "Fear not, for I have redeemed you; I have called you by your name; you are Mine. When you pass through the waters, I will be with you; and through the rivers, they shall not overflow you. When you walk through the fire, you shall not be burned, nor shall the flame scorch you. For I am the LORD your God, the Holy One of Israel, your Savior; I gave Egypt for your ransom, Ethiopia and Seba in your place. Since you were precious in My sight, you have been honored, and I have loved you; therefore I will give men for you, and people for your life. Fear not, for I am with you; I will bring your descendants from the east, and gather you from the west; I will say to the north, 'Give them up!' and to the south, 'Do not keep them back!' Bring My sons from afar, and My daughters from the ends of the earth—everyone who is called by My name, whom I have created for My glory; I have formed him, yes, I have made him."

———— *DECLARATION OF FAITH* ————

I have no cause to fear, for I am redeemed! God called to me personally, speaking my name and calling me His own. I belong to God. I am His own son/daughter and He loves me with all of His heart. When I pass through the troubles of life, He is with me. The raging rivers cannot sweep over me. I walk through fiery trials with confidence and emerge unharmed. I stand in the midst of Satan's fire shielded by God's hedge of protection. Not even the smell of the smoke can touch me.

The Lord is my Savior and my Father. He has redeemed me from the hand of bondage. I am precious and honored in His sight. He is very proud of me. His love for me spans the heavens and touches the very edges of the universe.

I have nothing to fear in my life, for God, the Creator of heaven and earth, is my Father and shield of protection for my household. He redeems my children for my sake and proclaims them to be blessed.

I have a covenant with God in which I am His own child and heir. He has adopted me, recreated me with a divine nature, and given me His own name. I am of God—called by His name and created for His glory.

(Romans 8:14-17; Job 1:10; Daniel 3:23-27; Psalms 5:11,12; 23:4,5; 103:17; Hebrews 2:14,15; 2 Corinthians 5:17; 2 Peter 1:4; John 17:22,23)

1 JOHN 4:15-18

Whoever confesses that Jesus is the Son of God, God abides in him, and he in God. And we have known and believed the love that God has for us. God is love, and he who abides in love abides in God, and God in him. Love has been perfected among us in this: that we may have boldness in the day of judgment; because as He is, so are we in this world. There is no fear in love; but perfect love casts out fear, because fear involves torment. But he who fears has not been made perfect in love.

——— *DECLARATION OF FAITH* ———

I acknowledge that Jesus is the Son of God; therefore, God lives in me and I in Him.

I both know and rely upon the love that God has for me.

God is love. As I live in God, I live in love, and God lives in me.

God's love is made complete in me so that I will have confidence in the day of judgment. As He is, so am I in this world. He is my example and my life. I purpose with all of my heart to be like Him in every way possible.

Therefore, I will allow no fear, terror, worry, or anxiety to enter my life for any reason whatsoever, for there is no fear in love. The perfect love that is within me drives out fear, because, in every case, fear has to do with punishment or torment of one kind or another. I do not need to fear the punishment of the curse [of the law of Moses], judgment for my sins, or eternal punishment in hell, for I have been redeemed!

God is on my side in any and every circumstance. He is always for me and never against me.

I will greet death with joy when my days are complete. It will be the homecoming that I have longed for.

So what do I have to fear? As I am in God, and made perfect in His love, fear becomes absolutely ridiculous to me.

(1 John 2:28; 4:7; 5:1,10-12; John 14:12; 2 Timothy 1:7; Joshua 1:5-9; 1 Peter 5:5-7; Romans 8:31; 1 Corinthians 15:54-58; Hebrews 10:14-17)

MATTHEW 8:26

But He said to them, "Why are you fearful, O you of little faith?" Then He arose and rebuked the winds and the sea, and there was a great calm.

——— *DECLARATION OF FAITH* ———

I reject all feelings of fear and speak words of faith to the adverse circumstances I am facing.

(Joshua 1:5-9; Mark 11:22-25; 2 Corinthians 4:13; Psalm 107:20,29)

DANIEL 10:10-13

Suddenly, a hand touched me, which made me tremble on my knees and on the palms of my hands. And he said to me, "O Daniel, man greatly beloved, understand the words that I speak to you, and stand upright, for I have now been sent to you." While he was speaking this word to me, I stood trembling. Then he said to me, "Do not fear, Daniel, for from the first day that you set your heart to understand, and to humble yourself before your God, your words were heard; and I have come because of your words. But the prince of the kingdom of Persia withstood me twenty-one days; and behold, Michael, one of the chief princes, came to help me, for I had been left alone there with the kings of Persia."

─────── *DECLARATION OF FAITH* ───────

God looks upon me with great favor and fills my life to overflowing with His blessings.

I humble myself under His mighty hand and He responds to me with tender compassion. His love compels me to move forward in courage and confidence. I refuse to allow fear to overwhelm me.

I am flooded with rivers of understanding as I acknowledge the Holy Spirit's presence within me. Through Him, I have an anointing to know exactly what to do in any given situation.

The principalities and powers of the devil's army pose no significant problem for me. God is within me and He has made me more than a conqueror to them.

My steadfast and persistent prayers open up a highway for the angels of God—freeing them to shower me with the blessings of heaven.

(Hebrews 1:14; 1 Peter 5:5-7; 2 Timothy 1:7; 1 Corinthians 2:6-16; John 16:13; Ephesians 6:10-18; 1 John 2:20,27)

Exodus 14:13-15

And Moses said to the people, "Do not be afraid. Stand still, and see the salvation of the LORD, which He will accomplish for you today. For the Egyptians whom you see today, you shall see again no more forever. The LORD will fight for you, and you shall hold your peace." And the LORD said to Moses, "Why do you cry to Me? Tell the children of Israel to go forward."

───── *DECLARATION OF FAITH* ─────

I fear nothing! I stand firm and confident under God's powerful hand. He works for me to produce a mighty salvation. I am still and at peace for I know that God, my heavenly Father, the Creator of the universe, loves me and fights on my behalf. Therefore, I will not allow fear to hold me back, but will go forward and conquer!

(Joshua 1:5-9; 2 Timothy 1:7; Romans 8:31-39; 2 Chronicles 20:15-24; Deuteronomy 1:30)

MARK 5:35,36

While He was still speaking, some came from the ruler of the synagogue's house who said, "Your daughter is dead. Why trouble the Teacher any further?" As soon as Jesus heard the word that was spoken, He said to the ruler of the synagogue, "Do not be afraid; only believe."

───── *DECLARATION OF FAITH* ─────

When I am faced with an evil report in the natural realm, I remain calm and continue to believe. I do not allow fear to rob me of what God has done for me. My faith brings to pass what I need, regardless of what is seen or known in the natural world.

(Numbers 14:1-9; 2 Timothy 1:6,7; Joshua 1:5-9; 2 Corinthians 5:7; Hebrews 11:1)

Deuteronomy 2:25

"'This day I will begin to put the dread and fear of you upon the nations under the whole heaven, who shall hear the report of you, and shall tremble and be in anguish because of you.'"

———— *DECLARATION OF FAITH* ————

This day my Father has put the fear and dread of me on all of my enemies. They shall hear His report of me and be in great anguish, for the Lord is on my side.

(James 4:7; 1 John 4:4; Romans 8:31; Luke 10:19; Exodus 23:22,27)

Deuteronomy 20:3,4

"And he shall say to them, 'Hear, O Israel: Today you are on the verge of battle with your enemies. Do not let your heart faint, do not be afraid, and do not tremble or be terrified because of them; for the LORD your God is He who goes with you, to fight for you against your enemies, to save you.'"

———— *DECLARATION OF FAITH* ————

I rush into battle against my enemies. I will not allow them to trespass on my Father's land. I boldly take the offensive, for I know the One in whom I believe and I am fully aware of His capabilities within me.

It is the Lord who goes before me. He is the first to confront the enemy on my behalf. I have nothing to fear. I refuse to give in to terror, trembling, or panic. The Lord fights for me and I stand in His victory!

(Exodus 14:13-15; Luke 10:19; Mark 3:27; 2 Timothy 1:12; Joshua 1:5-9; 1 Corinthians 15:57)

LUKE 8:24,25

And they came to Him and awoke Him, saying, "Master, Master, we are perishing!" Then He arose and rebuked the wind and the raging of the water. And they ceased, and there was a calm. But He said to them, "Where is your faith?"

─────── *DECLARATION OF FAITH* ───────

I am a man/woman of faith.

I reject all fear and anxiety in my life, casting it all on the shoulders of the One who bears my burdens. I am not seized by fear in any circumstance. I have the Word on my lips that covers and protects me in any situation.

I use my faith every hour of every day, believing and speaking to the problem, commanding the circumstance to get in line with the perfect will of God.

I am a victor here, not a victim, and I am in command of any given situation.

(Hebrews 11:6; 1 Peter 5:5-7; 2 Timothy 1:6,7; Matthew 11:28-30; Romans 8:37; 10:8; Psalm 119:93; Joshua 1:5-9; 2 Corinthians 4:13; Mark 11:23,24)

2 TIMOTHY 1:6-10

Therefore I remind you to stir up the gift of God which is in you through the laying on of my hands. For God has not given us a spirit of fear, but of power and of love and of a sound mind. Therefore do not be ashamed of the testimony of our Lord, nor of me His prisoner, but share with me in the sufferings for the gospel according to the power of God, who has saved us and called us with a holy calling, not according to our works, but according to His own purpose and grace which was given to us in Christ Jesus before time began, but has now been revealed by the appearing of our Savior Jesus Christ, who has abolished death and brought life and immortality to light through the gospel.

———— *DECLARATION OF FAITH* ————

I recognize that it is my responsibility to fan into flame the gift of God within me. I know that God has not given me a spirit of fear and cowardice, but of power (miraculous ability), love, and self-control. Therefore, I will remain perpetually on fire for Him, fully confident and always doing what He has called me to do.

I am not ashamed to testify about the Lord, for He has saved me and given me a holy calling, not because of anything that I have done to earn it, but because of His own purpose and grace.

According to God's sovereign plan, He chose me to receive His grace before the beginning of time. What an awesome thought it is to know that, even before the beginning of time, I held a special place in the heart of God. And now, through the appearing of my Lord and Savior Jesus Christ, who abrogated the death that was mine and brought me to life and immortality through the gospel, that grace that was once restrained has been poured out upon me in abundance.

(Ephesians 2:1-10; 5:18; 1 Timothy 4:14; Joshua 1:5-9; Acts 1:8; Matthew 3:11,12; Romans 1:16; Titus 3:4-7; 2 Thessalonians 2:13; John 3:16)

2 Kings 6:5,6

But as one was cutting down a tree, the iron ax head fell into the water; and he cried out and said, "Alas, master! For it was borrowed." So the man of God said, "Where did it fall?" And he showed him the place. So he cut off a stick, and threw it in there; and he made the iron float.

——— *DECLARATION OF FAITH* ———

I do not show fear in adverse circumstances. In whatever state I am in, I know that God is on my side and will provide the miracle that I need to see me through.

(Joshua 1:5-9; Deuteronomy 28:12; Hebrews 13:5,6; Romans 8:31; Philippians 4:11-19; 1 Peter 5:5-7)

1 PETER 5:5-7

"God resists the proud, but gives grace to the humble." Therefore humble yourselves under the mighty hand of God, that He may exalt you in due time, casting all your care upon Him, for He cares for you.

——— *DECLARATION OF FAITH* ———

It is written: "God resists the proud, but gives grace to the humble." Therefore, I clothe myself with humility towards my brothers and sisters in Christ.

I humble myself under God's mighty hand, knowing that He will exalt me in His perfect timing. I cast all of my fears, worries, and anxieties upon Him, for He cares for me deeply and will not allow me to be overcome by troubles and sorrow.

(Matthew 25:5-7; James 4:1-10; Philippians 4:6,7; Isaiah 43:1,2)

2 KINGS 19:6,7

And Isaiah said to them, "Thus you shall say to your master, 'Thus says the LORD: "Do not be afraid of the words which you have heard, with which the servants of the king of Assyria have blasphemed Me. Surely I will send a spirit upon him, and he shall hear a rumor and return to his own land; and I will cause him to fall by the sword in his own land."'"

──────── *DECLARATION OF FAITH* ────────

I have no fear of the words of the enemy and his underlings. My Father has delivered me with a sure and certain deliverance. When the enemy comes against me, he will fall by a sword from his own kingdom.

(Colossians 1:13; John 10:28,29; Psalms 2; 112:1-7; 2 Kings 19:35-37; 2 Chronicles 20:14-24)

1 CHRONICLES 17:25-27

"For You, O my God, have revealed to Your servant that You will build him a house. Therefore Your servant has found it in his heart to pray before You. And now, LORD, You are God, and have promised this goodness to Your servant. Now You have been pleased to bless the house of Your servant, that it may continue before You forever; for You have blessed it, O LORD, and it shall be blessed forever."

──────── *DECLARATION OF FAITH* ────────

I have confidence in my heavenly Father. He is on my side and I have no reason to fear. I have His Word that He will build my house in safety. My family—all of my posterity—is blessed. I rejoice in God's blessings upon my family, for I have this confidence: what the Lord blesses is blessed forever!

(Joshua 1:5-9; Romans 8:31; 1 Peter 5:5-7; Psalms 4:8; 103:17; Ephesians 1:3,13,14)

2 Chronicles 20:15-26

And he said, "Listen, all you of Judah and you inhabitants of Jerusalem, and you, King Jehoshaphat! Thus says the LORD to you: 'Do not be afraid nor dismayed because of this great multitude, for the battle is not yours, but God's. Tomorrow go down against them. They will surely come up by the Ascent of Ziz, and you will find them at the end of the brook before the Wilderness of Jeruel. You will not need to fight in this battle. Position yourselves, stand still and see the salvation of the LORD, who is with you, O Judah and Jerusalem!' Do not fear or be dismayed; tomorrow go out against them, for the LORD *is* with you." And Jehoshaphat bowed his head with his face to the ground, and all Judah and the inhabitants of Jerusalem bowed before the LORD, worshiping the LORD. Then the Levites of the children of the Kohathites and of the children of the Korahites stood up to praise the LORD God of Israel with voices loud and high. So they rose early in the morning and went out into the Wilderness of Tekoa; and as they went out, Jehoshaphat stood and said, "Hear me, O Judah and you inhabitants of Jerusalem: Believe in the LORD your God, and you shall be established; believe His prophets, and you shall prosper." And when he had consulted with the people, he appointed those who should sing to the LORD, and who should praise the beauty of holiness, as they went out before the army and were saying: "Praise the LORD, for His mercy endures forever." Now when they began to sing and to praise, the LORD set ambushes against the people of Ammon, Moab, and Mount Seir, who had come against Judah; and they were defeated. For the people of Ammon and Moab stood up against the inhabitants of

Mount Seir to utterly kill and destroy them. And when they had made an end of the inhabitants of Seir, they helped to destroy one another. So when Judah came to a place overlooking the wilderness, they looked toward the multitude; and there were their dead bodies, fallen on the earth. No one had escaped. When Jehoshaphat and his people came to take away their spoil, they found among them an abundance of valuables on the dead bodies, and precious jewelry, which they stripped off for themselves, more than they could carry away; and they were three days gathering the spoil because there was so much. And on the fourth day they assembled in the Valley of Berachah, for there they blessed the Lord; therefore the name of that place was called The Valley of Berachah until this day.

———— *DECLARATION OF FAITH* ————

I have set my face like flint to be true to the Lord. I hold fast to His promises and trust in the security of our covenant. Therefore, I remain confident that when the enemy attacks me with a great horde of allies bent on my destruction, the Lord shall stand to His feet and make His proclamation, "This battle is Mine!"

Whom shall I fear? Who can defeat my Father in heaven? He is the Lord of Hosts! I shall not be afraid! I shall take my position and stand my ground!

I listen for my Father's commands. I take heed to the voice of His prophets and I prosper in the midst of the turmoil. I praise His name for the victory, even in the heat of the battle. I give Him glory, for His mercy and loving-kindness endure forever!

I shall see the enemy fall in a great destruction, for the battle belongs to the Lord! Despite the battles that I must endure, my Father showers me with an endless supply of blessings.

(Deuteronomy 1:29,30; 20:14; 1 Samuel 14:20; 17:47; Exodus 3:22; 14:13,14; Numbers 14:9; Isaiah 7:9; Judges 7:22; 2 Corinthians 1:20; Romans 8:31; Psalms 91; 136; Luke 10:17-19; Genesis 12:1-3)

ISAIAH 51:11-16

So the ransomed of the LORD shall return, and come to Zion with singing, with everlasting joy on their heads. They shall obtain joy and gladness; sorrow and sighing shall flee away. "I, even I, am He who comforts you. Who are you that you should be afraid of a man who will die, and of the son of a man who will be made like grass? And you forget the LORD your Maker, who stretched out the heavens and laid the foundations of the earth; you have feared continually every day because of the fury of the oppressor, when he has prepared to destroy. And where is the fury of the oppressor? The captive exile hastens, that he may be loosed, that he should not die in the pit, and that his bread should not fail. But I am the LORD your God, who divided the sea whose waves roared—the LORD of hosts is His name. And I have put My words in your mouth; I have covered you with the shadow of My hand, that I may plant the heavens, lay the foundations of the earth, and say to Zion, 'You are My people.'"

——— *DECLARATION OF FAITH* ———

I am a citizen of Zion, God's holy church. I am ransomed and made whole. Everlasting joy crowns my head and gladness overtakes me, while sorrow and sighing flee away. It is God himself, the Creator of heaven and earth, who does this for me. He is an ever-present source of comfort in my life.

Fear is not an option when I acknowledge my Father's presence.

The oppressor is little more than an annoyance to me. I have been set free from his chains and made to be his master. I need never fear him again.

The prison bars that once closed me in have turned to twigs. And all of my needs, whether for power or provision, are continually met.

I am now a child of the King, born again under the name of almighty God. He has placed His Word on my lips, covered me with the shadow of His hand, and makes His declaration to all of creation that I am His.

(John 17:13-22; Hebrews 2:14-17; Colossians 2:13-15; 2 Timothy 1:7; Romans 10:8; Philippians 4:13-19)

PSALM 27:1-3

The LORD is my light and my salvation; whom shall I fear? The LORD is the strength of my life; of whom shall I be afraid? When the wicked came against me to eat up my flesh, my enemies and foes, they stumbled and fell. Though an army may encamp against me, my heart shall not fear; though war may rise against me, in this I will be confident.

──────── DECLARATION OF FAITH ────────

The Lord is my light and my salvation—I shall fear no one. The very Creator of the universe is the impenetrable fortress of safety in my life. For me to fear any enemy would be ludicrous.

When the enemy advances against me to devour my flesh, they will trip over their own devices and fall with a great destruction. Though a vast, innumerable army surrounds me, demanding my surrender, my heart will be still and I will not give in to terror. Even if they all attack at once and the odds appear overwhelming, I will still remain confident and full of courage for I know that my Father has taken His stand at my side. No matter what the odds may be, my victory is made certain and I will never give in to fear. I will never give in or give up.

(Psalms 18:28; 62:7; 84:11; Isaiah 12:2; 33:2; 60:19,20; Exodus 15:2; 2 Timothy 1:7)

Isaiah 54:13-17

All your children shall be taught by the LORD, and great shall be the peace of your children. In righteousness you shall be established; you shall be far from oppression, for you shall not fear; and from terror, for it shall not come near you. Indeed they shall surely assemble, but not because of Me. Whoever assembles against you shall fall for your sake. "Behold, I have created the blacksmith who blows the coals in the fire, who brings forth an instrument for his work; and I have created the spoiler to destroy. No weapon formed against you shall prosper, and every tongue which rises against you in judgment you shall condemn. This is the heritage of the servants of the LORD, and their righteousness is from Me," says the LORD.

—————— *DECLARATION OF FAITH* ——————

My children are taught by the Lord and He gives them tremendous peace and security.

My household is established in righteousness before Him and tyranny cannot gain a foothold in my life.

I have complete authority over all fear, anxiety, stress, and terror. I will not permit them in my life in any shape or form.

If I come under attack in any way, I know it is not the Lord's doing. All of His actions toward me are for good and never evil. It is He who gives me strength to conquer the enemy. Because of this, no weapon formed against me can prevail over me, and I thwart every accusation that comes against me.

This is part of my inheritance as God's son/daughter, and my righteousness and justification come from Him.

(Psalm 89:3,4; Jeremiah 29:11; 2 Timothy 1:7; Romans 5:1,2; 8:31,32,37)

PSALM 31:12-24

I am forgotten like a dead man, out of mind; I am like a broken vessel. For I hear the slander of many; fear is on every side; while they take counsel together against me, they scheme to take away my life. But as for me, I trust in You, O LORD; I say, "You are my God." My times are in Your hand; deliver me from the hand of my enemies, and from those who persecute me. Make Your face shine upon Your servant; save me for Your mercies' sake. Do not let me be ashamed, O LORD, for I have called upon You; let the wicked be ashamed; let them be silent in the grave. Let the lying lips be put to silence, which speak insolent things proudly and contemptuously against the righteous. Oh, how great is Your goodness, which You have laid up for those who fear You, which You have prepared for those who trust in You in the presence of the sons of men! You shall hide them in the secret place of Your presence from the plots of man; You shall keep them secretly in a pavilion from the strife of tongues. Blessed be the LORD, for He has shown me His marvelous kindness in a strong city! For I said in my haste, "I am cut off from before Your eyes"; nevertheless You heard the voice of my supplications when I cried out to You. Oh, love the LORD, all you His saints! For the LORD preserves the faithful, and fully repays the proud person. Be of good courage, and He shall strengthen your heart, all you who hope in the LORD.

─────── DECLARATION OF FAITH ───────

No matter what may happen in my life—even if my own sins have brought me to ruin and have made me a reproach among men—I will not lose faith nor forget that I am a born-again son/daughter of the living God. I am one of God's redeemed ones and my rights are secured by the blood of Jesus!

When fear encompasses me on every side and my enemies come against me to destroy me, I will remember who I am and who I believe in. My trust is in God alone for my victory. I will not retaliate against them but will give place to the vengeance of my Father. All of my days are in His hands, and He shall deliver me from my enemies and from those who persecute me.

He makes His face to shine upon me for His mercy's sake. For mercy's sake, He declares that I am perfect—free of all guilt. Therefore, the wicked who come against me shall be put to shame. They will be silent in their graves! Their proud and lying lips will be silenced, and their harsh words against me shall be seen as insolent stupidity.

My Father hides me in His secret place from the plots of man. He shields me in His pavilion and nullifies the words of the wicked.

He has preserved me and strengthened my heart. Forever I will praise His name!

(Galatians 3:1-13; 2 Kings 6:14-18; Hebrews 10:14; Psalm 91:1,2)

PSALM 56:3,4

Whenever I am afraid, I will trust in You. In God (I will praise His word), in God I have put my trust; I will not fear. What can flesh do to me?

——— DECLARATION OF FAITH ———

When fear comes against me to make me tremble with anxiety, I stand firm against it. My trust is in the Lord of Hosts. He is the King of kings and Lord of lords, the Almighty One, the El Shaddai who is more than enough to carry me. He is my Lord and my Savior—my faithful deliverer who takes His stand against all of my foes. He is faithful to me and has given me His Word that I shall not be harmed. Praise be to God and to the Word He has given me!

So what is there to be afraid of? Who can stand against the awesome power of God? With me, fear has become a joke! It makes absolutely no sense whatsoever.

(2 Timothy 1:7; 1 Peter 5:5-7; Psalm 91; Romans 8:31-39; Hebrews 13:5,6)

JAMES 1:2-8

My brethren, count it all joy when you fall into various trials, knowing that the testing of your faith produces patience. But let patience have its perfect work, that you may be perfect and complete, lacking nothing. If any of you lacks wisdom, let him ask of God, who gives to all liberally and without reproach, and it will be given to him. But let him ask in faith, with no doubting, for he who doubts is like a wave of the sea driven and tossed by the wind. For let not that man suppose that he will receive anything from the Lord; he is a double-minded man, unstable in all his ways.

——— *DECLARATION OF FAITH* ———

I consider it pure joy whenever I find myself facing trials and temptations [to give up on my faith] of every kind; for I know that the testing of my faith produces in me an enduring patience, and once this patience becomes an unfailing part of my character [when I am mature and complete in it], I will lack no good thing in my life.

I fully understand that Jesus has become my wisdom. God does not keep it from me, saying that I can't have it because I've done something wrong, but supplies it to me liberally, holding nothing back. All of His wisdom is rightfully mine in His name.

When I ask for wisdom, or anything else, I must not reason against my receiving it. A person who reasons against the promises of God is like a wave on the sea, driven and tossed about by whatever direction the wind might blow [or whichever way the circumstances may lead]. This type of person seldom receives anything from the Lord and cannot walk in his inheritance. They are double-minded and unstable in all of their ways.

I remain fixed and unwavering in my faith regardless of what my eyes may see, what my ears may hear, or what my body may feel, for I know that God is faithful and will fulfill His promise to me.

(Acts 5:41; Matthew 3:11,15,16; 5:10-12; 21:19-22; 2 Peter 1:6; Romans 5:3-5; 1 Corinthians 1:30; 2:6-16; Daniel 1:17,20; 2:22,23; Mark 11:22-25; Hebrews 6:12; Psalm 119:109-116; Jeremiah 29:11-13; James 4:8)

PROVERBS 1:33

"Whoever listens to me will dwell safely, and will be secure, without fear of evil."

────── *DECLARATION OF FAITH* ──────

I heed the ways of wisdom and live my life in safety. I am at peace—free from the fear that comes from an evil report.

(Numbers 14:8; Proverbs 3:24-26; Psalm 112:7)

PROVERBS 29:25

The fear of man brings a snare, but whoever trusts in the LORD shall be safe.

────── *DECLARATION OF FAITH* ──────

I do not allow fear to become a snare in my life. My complete and impenetrable trust is in my heavenly Father.

(2 Timothy 1:7; Genesis 12:12; 20:2; Luke 12:4; Joshua 1:5-9; John 12:42,43)

HAGGAI 2:2–9

"Speak now to Zerubbabel the son of Shealtiel, governor of Judah, and to Joshua the son of Jehozadak, the high priest, and to the remnant of the people, saying: 'Who is left among you who saw this temple in its former glory? And how do you see it now? In comparison with it, *is* this not in your eyes as nothing? Yet now be strong, Zerubbabel,' says the Lord; 'and be strong, Joshua, son of Jehozadak, the high priest; and be strong, all you people of the land,' says the Lord, 'and work; for I am with you,' says the Lord of hosts. 'According to the word that I covenanted with you when you came out of Egypt, so My Spirit remains among you; do not fear!' "For thus says the Lord of hosts: 'Once more (it *is* a little while) I will shake heaven and earth, the sea and dry land; and I will shake all nations, and they shall come to the Desire of All Nations, and I will fill this temple with glory,' says the Lord of hosts. 'The silver is Mine, and the gold *is* Mine,' says the Lord of hosts. 'The glory of this latter temple shall be greater than the former,' says the Lord of hosts. 'And in this place I will give peace,' says the Lord of hosts."

DECLARATION OF FAITH

I am strong in the Lord and in the power of His might. I will work in His name and produce wonderful things for His glory. He is with me at all times. His Spirit dwells within me, leading me on the path of victory.

With God on my side, fear is not an option. It is a preposterous and ludicrous prospect. My Father has declared that I am to be at peace—in perfect comfort and safety—free from stress, terror, and anxiety.

This earth belongs to my Father and I am His heir. He has shaken the world and established His church. He has appointed for me my part and my portion. He has filled me with His glory and stabilizes me as His representative.

I refuse to hang on to empty religion with its false humility. It is time for the earth to know and see the glory of God's children!

(Ephesians 6:10; John 16:13; Colossians 3:17; Hebrews 13:5,6; 1 Corinthians 15:57; Romans 8:14-17; 31; 2 Timothy 1:6,7; Philippians 4:7-9; Galatians 4:5,6; Psalms 24:1; 112:1-10; 2 Corinthians 5:17-21; Genesis 13:2)

ISAIAH 41:8-20

"But you, Israel, are My servant, Jacob whom I have chosen, the descendants of Abraham My friend. You whom I have taken from the ends of the earth, and called from its farthest regions, and said to you, 'You *are* My servant, I have chosen you and have not cast you away: Fear not, for I am with you; be not dismayed, for I am your God. I will strengthen you, yes, I will help you, I will uphold you with My righteous right hand.' Behold, all those who were incensed against you shall be ashamed and disgraced; they shall be as nothing, and those who strive with you shall perish. You shall seek them and not find them—those who contended with you. Those who war against you shall be as nothing, as a nonexistent thing. For I, the LORD your God, will hold your right hand, saying to you, 'Fear not, I will help you.' Fear not, you worm Jacob, you men of Israel! I will help you," says the LORD and your Redeemer, the Holy One of Israel. "Behold, I will make you into a new threshing sledge with sharp teeth; you shall thresh the mountains and beat them small, and make the hills like chaff. You shall winnow them, the wind shall carry them away, and the whirlwind shall scatter them; you shall rejoice in the LORD, and glory in the Holy One of Israel. The poor and needy seek water, but there is none, their tongues fail for thirst. I, the LORD, will hear them; I, the God of Israel, will not forsake them. I will open rivers in desolate heights, and fountains in the midst of the valleys; I will make the wilderness a pool of water, and the dry land springs of water. I will plant in the wilderness the cedar and the acacia tree, the myrtle and the oil tree; I will set in the desert the cypress tree and the pine and the box tree together, that they may see and know, and consider and understand together, that the hand of the LORD has done this, and the Holy One of Israel has created it."

─── DECLARATION OF FAITH ───

I am a descendent of Abraham, the father of my faith. God loves me with all of His heart and has chosen me out from among all of the people of the earth to be His own son/daughter.

I have no cause for fear, for my God is with me. I will not be dismayed, for God is my Father and He has promised to never leave me nor forsake me. He strengthens me and assists me in every circumstance. He upholds me with His righteous right hand so that my victory is made certain.

All who rage against me shall be disgraced and put to shame. Those who oppose me shall come to nothing and their cause against me shall be eliminated. When I look about me for a formidable foe, a strong enemy and worthy opponent, I find none. The greater One is within me and He makes all of my enemies seem like harmless bugs in my presence.

*The Lord, God of heaven and earth, takes hold of my right hand and says to me, "Son/Daughter, don't you worry about a thing. I've got your back and won't allow anything to harm you. I'm always here for you to help you with anything you need. So don't be afraid. Think about it, son/daughter, **I am your Father**. You belong to Me and I belong to you. Is there **ever** a reason to be afraid? I have redeemed you and recreated you. You are a new creation in Christ Jesus, a threshing sledge, new and sharp, with many teeth; a fierce warrior and fearsome prince/princess in My kingdom. For you, no task is too difficult and no foe unconquerable. So rejoice, My son/daughter. Enjoy My presence in your life. I will always be with you. I promise you that you will never go thirsty again. I will answer your every prayer and never abandon you—no child, not for any reason. I will make rivers flow on your barren heights and turn your desert places into pools of water. All that you have I will bless for your sake. Yes, son/daughter, for **your** sake. I want all the world to know how much I love you—how proud I am of you—and what joy you bring to My heart. I love you, son/daughter. Never forget that."*

(Galatians 3:7; Psalm 2; 1 Corinthians 15:57; Deuteronomy 11:25; Hebrews 13:5,6; John 6:35-40; Colossians 2:9-15)

OTHER RECOMMENDED MATERIALS

The Holy Spirit is within you right now, granting you the very ability to communicate with the Father. That means no matter where you are or what you are doing, you can speak with Him and hear what He has to say.

I highly recommend that you read every book you can on learning to hear from God. Get the book *To Know Him*[1] by Gloria Copeland (popular Bible teacher and best-selling author) and read it over and over again. Her tape series, "Living Contact"[2] is another good resource. Get *The Complete Personalized Promise Bible for Men*[3] or *Women*[4] and speak all of those promises on God being your friend and closest companion. Find all of those places in the Word where other believers experienced fellowship with God. And remember, test all things and hold fast to that which is good. God never deviates from His own Word.

I highly recommend that you learn more about how to take care of your body properly. God has placed several brilliant and anointed men and women in the body of Christ to help us in this area. Any books, tapes, or other information you can get by Dr. Jordan Rubin, Dr. Don Colbert, Dr. Ted Broer, or Dr. Valerie Saxion would be a good place to start.

I love you in the Lord, and I'm looking forward to that day when we meet in heaven and I can hug your neck and spend time hearing about all the good things God has done for you. Always know that you have a brother in El Paso, Texas, who is praying for you and truly cares about your success in life. May God bless you abundantly this day and every day, now and forevermore.

TOPICAL INDEX

God's Willingness to Heal You

Exodus 15:26; Deuteronomy 7:12-16; 1 Kings 8:33-40; 2 Kings 20:1-6;
2 Chronicles 30:13-20; Psalms 16:5-9; 21:2-4; 27:13,14; 34:17-19; 91:9-16;
107:17-22; 119:65-68; Isaiah 19:21,22; 35:1-6; 41:10; 42:5-7; Jeremiah 33:6-9;
Matthew 8:1-4; 8:5-13; 14:14; Mark 1:40-42; 8:22-25; Luke 5:12,13;
John 9:1-7.

When You Are Told You Are Going to Die

Deuteronomy 28:15-68; 1 Kings 17:17-24; 2 Kings 20:1-6; Psalms 13:3-6;
27:13,14; 30:1-5; 38:3-22; 41:1-3; 73:26; 79:11; 91:9-16; 92:12-15; 103:1-5;
107:17-22; 118:16,17; 128:1-6; Proverbs 3:1,2,7,8; 4:20-27; Isaiah 53:1-6;
Matthew 9:18-25; Mark 5:22-43; Luke 7:2-10; 8:41-55; John 4:46-53;
Romans 4:16-21.

Aids

Deuteronomy 7:12-16; 28:15-68; 1 Kings 17:17-24; 2 Kings 20:1-6;
Psalms 6:1-10; 13:3-6; 27:13,14; 30:1-5; 38:3-22; 41:1-3; 73:26; 79:11;
91:9-16; 92:12-15; 103:1-5; 107:17-22; 118:16,17; 128:1-6; Proverbs 3:1,2,7,8;
4:20-27; Isaiah 53:1-6; Matthew 9:18-25; Mark 5:22-43; Luke 7:2-10; 8:41-55;
John 4:46-53; Romans 4:16-21.

Attitude

Psalms 128:1-6; 146:5-8; Proverbs 3:13-18; 14:30; 17:22; 18:14; 18:20,21.

Blindness

Exodus 4:11; Deuteronomy 7:12-16; 28:15-68; Psalm 146:5-8; Isaiah 35:1-6; 42:5-7; Matthew 9:27-30; 11:4-6; 12:22; 15:30,31; 20:30-34; 21:14; Mark 8:22-25; 10:46-52; Luke 4:17-27; 7:20-23; 18:35-43; John 5:1-17; 9:1-7.

Broken Heart

Deuteronomy 28:15-68; Psalms 6:1-10; 16:5-9; 30:1-5; 34:17-19; 38:3-22; 73:26; 146:5-8; 147:1-3; Proverbs 14:30; 17:22; 18:14; Isaiah 61:1-3; Ezekiel 34:1-4; 34:11-16; 47:8-12; Luke 4:17-27.

Cancer

Deuteronomy 7:12-16; 28:15-68; 1 Kings 17:17-24; 2 Kings 20:1-6; Psalms 6:1-10; 13:3-6; 27:13,14; 30:1-5; 38:3-22; 41:1-3; 73:26; 79:11; 91:9-16; 92:12-15; 103:1-5; 107:17-22; 118:16,17; 128:1-6; Proverbs 3:1,2,7,8; 4:20-27; Isaiah 53:1-6; Matthew 9:18-25; Mark 5:22-43; Luke 7:2-10; 8:41-55; John 4:46-53; Romans 4:16-21.

Children

Exodus 23:25,26; Deuteronomy 4:40; 5:16; 5:20; 12:28; 28:15-68; 30:14-20; Psalms 91:9-16; 92:12-15; 107:17-22; 128:1-6; 147:1-3; Mark 5:22-43; 9:17-29; John 4:46-53; 2 John 1:2-4.

Circulation and Blood Flow Problems

Deuteronomy 28:15-68; Psalms 27:13,14; 38:3-22; 73:26; 107:17-22; Proverbs 14:30; Matthew 9:18-25; Mark 5:22-43; Luke 8:41-55.

Community Illnesses

Exodus 15:26; 23:25,26; Deuteronomy 7:12-16; 28:15-68; 1 Kings 8:33-40; Psalms 6:1-10; 16:5-9; 38:3-22; 91:9-16; Acts 4:23-31.

Deafness

Exodus 4:11; Deuteronomy 7:12-16; 28:15-68; Isaiah 35:1-6; Matthew 11:4-6; Mark 9:17-29; Luke 7:20-23.

Demonic Influence

Deuteronomy 28:15-68; 1 Kings 8:33-40; Psalms 6:1-10; 13:3-6; 30:1-5; 38:3-22; 41:1-3; 91:9-16; Jeremiah 30:12-17; Matthew 4:23,24; 8:16,17; 10:1; 10:7,8; 12:22; 15:22-28; Mark 1:32-34; 3:14,15; 6:7,12,13; 9:17-29; 16:14-20; Luke 7:20-23; 9:1-6; 9:11; 10:17-20; 13:31,32.

Depression

Deuteronomy 28:15-68; Psalms 6:1-10; 16:5-9; 30:1-5; 34:17-19; 38:3-22; 73:26; 146:5-8; 147:1-3; Proverbs 14:30; 17:22; 18:14; Isaiah 61:1-3; Ezekiel 34:1-4; 34:11-16; 47:8-12; Luke 4:17-27.

Emotional Issues

Deuteronomy 28:15-68; Psalms 6:1-10; 16:5-9; 30:1-5; 34:17-19; 38:3-22; 73:26; 146:5-8; 147:1-3; Proverbs 14:30; 17:22; 18:14; Isaiah 61:1-3; Ezekiel 34:1-4; 34:11-16; 47:8-12; Luke 4:17-27.

Fear

Deuteronomy 28:15-68; 30:14-20; 2 Kings 20:1-6; Psalms 21:2-4; 27:13,14; 91:9-16; Isaiah 35:1-6; 41:10; 57:15-19; Ezekiel 47:8-12; Mark 5:22-43; Luke 1:37,38,45; 8:41-55; 2 Corinthians 12:7-10.

_____

Fertility

Genesis 20:17; Exodus 23:25,26; Deuteronomy 7:12-16; 28:15-68; Psalms 92:12-15; 128:1-6.

_____

Fever

Deuteronomy 28:15-68; Psalms 6:1-10; 38:3-22; Matthew 8:14,15; Mark 1:30,31; Luke 4:38-40; John 4:46-53; Acts 28:8,9.

_____

Flu

Exodus 15:26; 23:25,26; Deuteronomy 7:12-16; 28:15-68; 1 Kings 8:33-40; Psalms 6:1-10; 16:5-9; 38:3-22; 91:9-16; Acts 4:23-31.

_____

Hearing Problems

Exodus 4:11; Deuteronomy 7:12-16; 28:15-68; Isaiah 35:1-6; Matthew 11:4-6; Mark 9:17-29; Luke 7:20-23.

_____

Heart Problems

Deuteronomy 28:15-68; Psalms 27:13,14; 38:3-22; 73:26; 107:17-22; Proverbs 14:30; Matthew 9:18-25; Mark 5:22-43; Luke 8:41-55.

Incurable Diseases

Deuteronomy 7:12-16; 28:15-68; 1 Kings 17:17-24; 2 Kings 20:1-6;
Psalms 6:1-10; 13:3-6; 27:13,14; 30:1-5; 38:3-22; 41:1-3; 73:26; 79:11;
91:9-16; 92:12-15; 103:1-5; 107:17-22; 118:16,17; 128:1-6; Proverbs 3:1,2,7,8;
4:20-27; Isaiah 53:1-6; Matthew 9:18-25; Mark 5:22-43; Luke 7:2-10; 8:41-55;
John 4:46-53; Romans 4:16-21.

Insanity

Deuteronomy 28:15-68; Proverbs 14:30; 17:22; Matthew 4:23,24;
Mark 6:7,12,13; 9:17-29; Luke 6:17-19; 10:17-20; Hebrews 12:12,13.

Intercession for Others Who Need Healing

Genesis 20:17; Numbers 12:10-15; Deuteronomy 28:15-68; 1 Kings 8:33-40;
17:17-24; 2 Chronicles 30:13-20; Isaiah 58:6-11; Proverbs 10:11; 12:18;
Mark 6:4-6; 16:14-20; Luke 4:38-40; 5:12,13; Acts 4:23-31; 5:14-16; 19:11,12;
28:8,9; James 5:13-16.

Leprosy

Numbers 12:10-15; 2 Kings 5:1-14; Matthew 8:1-4; 10:7,8; 11:4-6;
Luke 4:17-27; 7:20-23; 17:12-20.

Long Life

Genesis 24:1; Exodus 23:25,26; Deuteronomy 4:40; 5:16; 5:32,33; 28:15-68;
30:14-20; 2 Kings 20:1-6; Psalms 13:3-6; 21:2-4; 30:1-5; 79:11; 91:9-16;
92:12-15; 128:1-6; Proverbs 3:1,2,7,8; 3:13-18; Luke 8:41-55.

Medicine

Deuteronomy 12:28; 1 Kings 8:33-40; 2 Chronicles 7:14-16; Psalms 103:1-5; 107:17-22; 128:1-6; Proverbs 2:10,11; 3:1,2,7,8; 3:13-18; 4:20-27; Ezekiel 47:8-12; 1 Timothy 5:23.

Mind Conditions

Deuteronomy 28:15-68; Proverbs 14:30; 17:22; Matthew 4:23,24; Mark 6:7,12,13; 9:17-29; Luke 6:17-19; 10:17-20; Hebrews 12:12,13.

Nutrition, Medicine, and Natural Remedies

Deuteronomy 12:28; 1 Kings 8:33-40; 2 Chronicles 7:14-16; Psalms 103:1-5; 107:17-22; 128:1-6; Proverbs 2:10,11; 3:1,2,7,8; 3:13-18; 4:20-27; Ezekiel 47:8-12; 1 Timothy 5:23.

Plague

Exodus 15:26; 23:25,26; Deuteronomy 7:12-16; 28:15-68; 1 Kings 8:33-40; Psalms 6:1-10; 16:5-9; 38:3-22; 91:9-16; Acts 4:23-31.

Psychosis

Deuteronomy 28:15-68; Proverbs 14:30; 17:22; Matthew 4:23,24; Mark 6:7,12,13; 9:17-29; Luke 6:17-19; 10:17-20; Hebrews 12:12,13.

Schizophrenia

Deuteronomy 28:15-68; Proverbs 14:30; 17:22; Matthew 4:23,24; Mark 6:7,12,13; 9:17-29; Luke 6:17-19; 10:17-20; Hebrews 12:12,13.

Skin Diseases

Numbers 12:10-15; 2 Kings 5:1-14; Matthew 8:1-4; 10:7,8; 11:4-6; Luke 4:17-27; 7:20-23; 17:12-20.

Speech Impediments; Muteness

Exodus 4:11; Deuteronomy 7:12-16; 28:15-68; Psalm 38:3-22; Isaiah 35:1-6; Matthew 12:22; 15:30,31; Mark 9:17-29.

Vision Problems

Exodus 4:11; Deuteronomy 7:12-16; 28:15-68; Psalm 146:5-8; Isaiah 35:1-6; 42:5-7; Matthew 9:27-30; 11:4-6; 12:22; 15:30,31; 20:30-34; 21:14; Mark 8:22-25; 10:46-52; Luke 4:17-27; 7:20-23; 18:35-43; John 5:1-17; 9:1-7.

ENDNOTES

Introduction

1. Based on definitions from Brown, Driver, Briggs and Gesenius, *The KJV Old Testament Hebrew Lexicon,* "Hebrew Lexicon entry for Shalowm, available from <http://www.biblestudytools.net/Lexicons/Hebrew/heb.cgi?number=7 965&version=kjv>, s.v. "shalom."

2. Ibid.

Exodus 15:26, Prayer

1. Brown, Driver, Briggs and Gesenius, "Hebrew Lexicon entry for Rapha," available from http://www.biblestudytools.net/Lexicons/Hebrew/heb.cgi?number=7495&version=kjv, s.v. "heal," Exodus 15:26. The first time God revealed Himself as Jehovah Rapha was through Moses during the journey in the wilderness.

Isaiah 33:24, Declaration of Faith

1. This is not talking about denying the circumstances, but rather choosing to speak what the Word says about them instead of speaking the problems.

Mark 16:14-20, Prayer and Declaration of Faith

1. This declaration of trampling on serpents and drinking deadly things without being harmed is not suggesting that you randomly go out and try this, although the occasion may arise in ministry or missions work that this might be the case to help further the gospel, as it was with the apostle Paul in Acts 28:4-6. In the spiritual sense,

this is referring to God's protection over our lives. As Matthew Henry says, "[We] shall be kept unhurt by that generation of vipers among whom [we] live, and by the malice of the old serpent [the devil]." *Matthew Henry's Commentary on the Whole Bible,* "Commentary on Mark 16," available from <http://bible.cross-walk.com/Commentaries/ MatthewHenryComplete/mhc-com.cgi? book=mr&chapter=016>, s.v. "Mark 16:14-18."

[2] Ibid.

[3] Ibid.

---

1 Timothy 5:23, Reference

[1] At first glance, all I thought about was that Paul was telling Timothy to drink wine. The more I looked at the verse, the more I began to see why it was in the Bible.

First of all, Timothy was drinking plenty of water in order to replenish his system and keep it at the optimum performance level. But still he was experiencing some health problems. Did Paul tell him to just pray and the problems would all go away? No. Certainly God would answer the prayer and heal him, but then a month later the ailment would return because Timothy needed something additional in his system. Therefore, Paul told him to take a supplement. Studies show that red wine extract has incredible antioxidant effects on the body. When Paul wrote to Timothy, the supplement he recommended was red wine. Today we can get the same effect, and even better, in the form of a vitamin.

These days the food we eat does not have nearly the nutritional value that it once did. Therefore, we should supplement our diets with a good, daily multivitamin and mineral regimen.

Having said that, I want to warn you to be careful of what supplements you take. Some supplements can interfere with the effects of certain medications. Therefore, if you are on any medication, you should consult your physician before going on any vitamin regimen.

Hebrews 12:12,13, Declaration of Faith

[1] "The Father of our spirits never grieves willingly...his own children. It is always for our profit; and the advantage he intends us thereby is no less than our being partakers of his holiness; it is to correct and cure those sinful disorders which make us unlike to God, and to improve and to increase those graces which are the image of God in us, that we may be and act more like our heavenly Father." Matthew Henry, available from http://bible.crosswalk.com/Commentaries/MatthewHenryComplete/mhc-com.cgi?book=heb&chapter=012, s.v. "Hebrews 12:12,13."

Other Recommended Materials

[1] Gloria Copeland, *To Know Him* (Tulsa, Oklahoma: Harrison House Publishers, 2005).

[2] "Living Contact" is available from http://kcm.org/usstore/advanced_search_result.php?keywords=Living+Contact&osCsid=fce1624e84d62e858a0e605af8e87196.

[3] James R. Riddle, *The Complete Personalized Promise Bible for Men* (Tulsa, Oklahoma: Harrison House Publishers, 2005).

[4] Ibid., *The Complete Personalized Promise Bible for Women*.

PRAYER OF SALVATION

God loves you—no matter who you are, no matter what your past. God loves you so much that He gave His one and only begotten Son for you. The Bible tells us that "...whoever believes in him shall not perish but have eternal life" (John 3:16 NIV). Jesus laid down His life and rose again so that we could spend eternity with Him in heaven and experience His absolute best on earth. If you would like to receive Jesus into your life, say the following prayer out loud and mean it from your heart.

Heavenly Father, I come to You admitting that I am a sinner. Right now, I choose to turn away from sin, and I ask You to cleanse me of all unrighteousness. I believe that Your Son, Jesus, died on the cross to take away my sins. I also believe that He rose again from the dead so that I might be forgiven of my sins and made righteous through faith in Him. I call upon the name of Jesus Christ to be the Savior and Lord of my life. Jesus, I choose to follow You and ask that You fill me with the power of the Holy Spirit. I declare that right now I am a child of God. I am free from sin and full of the righteousness of God. I am saved in Jesus' name. Amen.

If you prayed this prayer to receive Jesus Christ as your Savior for the first time, please contact us on the Web at **www.harrisonhouse.com** to receive a free book.

Or you may write to us at

Harrison House
P.O. Box 35035
Tulsa, Oklahoma 74153

ABOUT THE AUTHOR

James Riddle is a successful entrepreneur, educator, and Bible teacher. His unique approach to writing stirs the heart and encourages the soul. One does not have to sit under his teaching for long to know that he has a deep love for the body of Christ. It is pure joy for him to see God's children living in closeness with their Father and fulfilling the call He has on their lives.

At the center of all of James' success is his love for the Word. "In my own personal life," he says, "I have a simple mission statement. 'Be the person you are created to be.'" It is his resolute conviction that only through the Word can anyone achieve true success and be the person that God wants them to be. Therefore, the Word must always be our final authority no matter what we are facing.

It is just that attitude that caused James to write *The Complete Personalized Promise Bible* Series. For three and a half years he researched and personalized everything the Bible says about who we are, what we have, and how we are supposed to act as Christians. It was birthed in a determination to believe the right things so he could keep his prayers in the perfect will of God. All of that research and dedication is now available to the public, and what a blessing it is!

James holds an honors degree in Creative Writing from the University of Texas at El Paso. His *Complete Personalized Promise Bible* series has sold well over 100,000 copies. He is the father of four and lovingly refers to his wife, Jinny, as his beautiful Puerto Rican princess.

James Riddle would love to hear how God has blessed you through this material. Please send your testimony to the following address:

James Riddle Ministries
P.O. Box 972624
El Paso, Texas 79997

Or e-mail him at:
thepromisecenter@elp.rr.com

Visit James Riddle online at:
www.jamesriddle.net

DISCOVER GOD'S PURPOSE AND PROMISES FOR YOUR FINANCIAL LIFE!

For the first time, you can find every promise from God's Word about your financial life in one handy resource. You'll find every Bible promise on finances along with a powerful declaration of faith and a conversational prayer for you to speak directly from your heart to the heart of God. Selected topics include:

Debt

Generosity

Success

Investing

Saving

Crises

Budgeting

Greed

Ministry

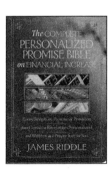

This simple yet potent tool will help you unleash the power of faith and prayer in your life right now and help you receive the financial blessings God has for you today.

1-57794-779-7

Available at fine bookstores everywhere or visit www.harrisonhouse.com.

EVERY SINGLE PROMISE FROM GENESIS TO REVELATION PERSONALIZED JUST FOR YOU!

The original *Complete Personalized Promise Bible* gives you every promise in the Bible, chronologically organized from Genesis to Revelation and personalized with a declaration of faith! There is no other book that contains the 1,800-plus promises from God's Word written just for you and your life. By studying these promises and praying them back to your Father God, you will establish your faith for those promises to be a part of your life. Inspiring introductions are included for each book of the Bible and an extensive topical index gives you a handy resource for all the challenges of life!

 **ISBN 1-57794-537-9**

Available at fine bookstores everywhere or visit www.harrisonhouse.com.

ALL THE PROMISES FOR WOMEN IN AN EASY-TO-USE TOPICAL FORMAT!

Now women can find every promise in the Bible by topic in this specially designed edition. Each Scripture is personalized just like the original version and includes inspiring devotional introductions to each topic. Selected topics include:

Freedom From Fear

Encouragement

Long Life

A Successful Marriage

Children

Peace

Protection

And more!

This unique and inspiring book is perfect as a treasured gift for yourself or someone you love.

 **ISBN 1-57794-664-2**

Available at fine bookstores everywhere or visit www.harrisonhouse.com.

EVERY PROMISE IN THE BIBLE IN TOPICAL FORMAT JUST FOR MEN!

This easy-to-use topical edition for men gives them all the promises specially designed for their needs. Each Scripture is personalized just like the original version and includes inspiring devotional introductions to each topic. Selected topics include:

Your Call to Leadership

Guidance

Faith

Prosperity

Knowing Your Destiny in Life

Wisdom

And more!

A powerful and life-changing gift, this unique book is perfect for yourself and others!

 **1-57794-663-4**

Available at fine bookstores everywhere or visit www.harrisonhouse.com.